The Wilson Farm

Country Cookbook

⋀ ADDISON-WESLEY PUBLISHING COMPANY, INC.

Reading, Massachusetts   Menlo Park, California

Don Mills, Ontario   Wokingham, England   Amsterdam

Sydney   Singapore   Tokyo   Mexico City   Bogotá

Santiago   San Juan

The Wilson Farm

Country Cookbook

Recipes from New England's Favorite Farm Stand

Lynne Wilson

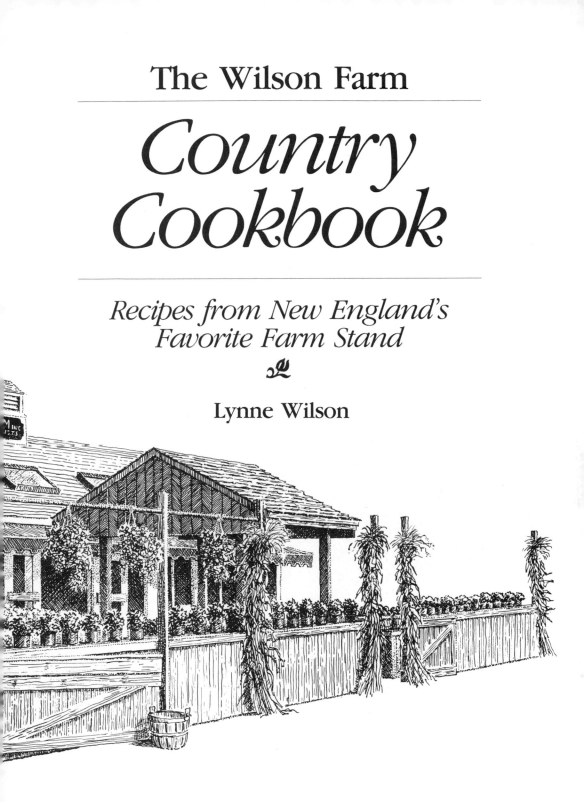

Library of Congress Cataloging in Publication Data

Wilson, Lynne.
 The Wilson Farm country cookbook.

 Includes index.
 1. Cookery, American—New England style. I. Title.
TX715.W75124 1985   641.5974   84-24408
ISBN 0–201–09676–5
ISBN 0–201–09677–3 (pbk.)

Illustrations by Dana Gaines

Text design by Janis Capone
Set in 11-point ITC Garamond Book by DEKR Corporation

ISBN 0–201–09676–5 H
         09677–3 P

Ninth Printing, September 2001

I dedicate this book

To my husband, Alan, daughter, Lesley, and son, Scott, with many thanks for their understanding, love, and support during the past months when I was either in the kitchen or at my typewriter.

To my mother, Nan Culler, who showed tremendous patience when I was a child creating chaos by cooking in her kitchen, and to my father, Raymond Culler, who always willingly ate the results of that chaos.

Without the encouragement, past and present, of all of them, this book would not have been written.

Contents

Acknowledgments

*E*veryone at *Wilson Farm* willingly (joyfully, when taste-testing) helped me with the book. Every time I arrived at the farm in my white apron, I was greeted with grins, since it was obvious that food was on the way. When I brought my samples, I felt like the Pied Piper, as I always had a following of would-be tasters. Many of the crew ate vegetables they had never tried before, and I learned a great deal about their personal food preferences. There were soup people, dessert people, vegetable people, lovers (and connoisseurs) of Italian-style cooking, and so forth, and so forth. In the office, Nancy MacLauchlan liked everything, but especially soup. Meg Stewart, when she wasn't frantically typing the final manuscript, enjoyed anything that wasn't spicy. Cindy Wilson even tried some of the recipes on her friends and reported their reactions to me. Peter Oprea set up the display for the cover photograph at the farm stand. Keith Hutchins, a good cook himself, offered great suggestions, but his brother, Carl, was trying not to eat between meals. He was successful until I brought in a pot filled with cooked shell beans. I had found Carl's weakness. Some people can't resist chocolate, but Carl can't resist shell beans. On the farm itself, Arthur Ford liked everything, but especially the stew. I think, if the truth were known, he is a meat-and-potatoes man. I was sorry that Calvin Wilson, who lives and works on the New Hampshire farm, was seldom in Lexington when I was experimenting with the recipes. However, when he was here, he tried anything.

For some reason, inexplicable even to me, I left the first chapter, Appetizers, to last when I was testing my recipes. Fortunately, my sister, Connie Falconer, came to visit from her home in Indonesia as I was working on that chapter. Her enthusiastic help — chopping onions, washing dishes, and especially tasting and commenting — gave me a boost when I had "run out of steam" toward the end of writing the book.

My good friend Marian Morash, author of *The Victory Garden Cookbook,* was extremely encouraging when I was considering writing this book, as was my husband. Alan, who always has more faith in me than I have in myself, has been tremendously supportive. Now that the book is completed, I'll miss hearing my nephew Chris Fuery yell across the farm, "What's cooking, Aunt Lynne?" knowing that he's hungry and looking for samples. His brother, Steve, who is not a vegetable lover, teased me about writing a pizza chapter for him, but he was a sport and even sampled the vegetable dishes.

To these people and the rest of the staff at the farm, I say thank you for your support. Ours is a family farm, but it is an extended family, because many of our employees have worked with us for years, and many of our customers have been shopping with us since we opened our first farm stand in 1953. Customers, staff, and family have all been interested and helpful in this project, and I am grateful to each of them for their encouragement.

Introduction

W*hen I decided* to write this cookbook, I wanted to include a brief history of Wilson Farm. This was not a simple task, as no farm records are available. I was aware that the valley area we now call Wilson Farm had been farmed since Revolutionary times, so I hoped to discover, among other facts, what crops were grown and animals raised then. After much research, I discovered that Lexington was a dairy farming area from the 1700s and a large producer of milk into the early twentieth century. I don't know why the Wilsons chose to become market gardeners rather than dairy farmers, but I found some interesting statistics in the old town directories. In 1884, when the Wilson brothers started farming on Pleasant Street, the directory listed seventeen milk dealers. In the next available directory, which was dated 1899, that number had increased to twenty-three, and eleven market gardeners, including James Alexander Wilson of Pleasant Street, were also listed.

My husband's grandfather James Alexander Wilson emigrated from Ireland with a brother and sister in 1880, when he was eighteen years old. They came to work for their uncle, who was a farmer on Bow Street in Lexington. In 1884 the sister left Lexington, and the two brothers started out on their own, renting part of the present farm on Pleasant Street. Subsequently, James Alexander's brother moved to Lowell to work in the textile business. James Alexander remained on the farm in Lexington, raising a family of three boys and three girls. Two of the boys, Walter and Stanley, stayed on the farm. Their sons, Donald and Alan, are the present owners. Stanley had only one child, Donald. Donald and his wife, Betty, have two children, James and Calvin. Walter had two children, Barbara and Alan. Barbara and her husband, Francis Fuery, have three children, Nancy, Christopher, and Stephen. Alan and I have two children, Lesley and Scott. All seven of these children presently work at the farm in various jobs. Donald's children, the oldest cousins, have joined the business on a full-time basis.

Although Wilson Farm in Lexington, Massachusetts, has been farmed by Wilsons for over one hundred years, Lexington was an established farming community long before the Wilsons arrived. It was settled some time prior to 1642 as part of Cambridge and was known as Cambridge Farms. It wasn't until 1713 that Lexington was incorporated as a separate town and renamed. Our farm was part of a larger one owned by the Brown family during the eighteenth and nineteenth centuries. The original Brown farmhouse still stands on the Massachusetts Avenue side of the farm. This road was the route taken by Paul Revere and, a short time later, by the British prior to the famous Battle of Lexington on April 19, 1775.

James Alexander Wilson rented and eventually bought the farm from a Miss Fiske, a descendant of the Brown family. I discovered in the town assessors' records that James Alexander had a very small farming operation when he began in 1884 — he was taxed only for two horses. By the next year he had increased his holdings and paid taxes on two horses and four cows. He grew vegetables and feed for the cows, using the horses both to farm and to pull the produce wagon to market. At that time farmers from Lexington, Concord, Bedford, and other nearby towns took their produce to Boston to sell at Quincy Market.

James Alexander grew cabbage, white turnip, celery, carrots, and beets, some of which he stored in earth pits through the winter months. Periodically, during the winter and early spring, he sold some of his stored produce at market. He was well known for the quality of the Pascal celery he raised, the beginning of a tradition of quality that Wilson Farm has always tried to preserve.

About 1920, James Alexander turned the farm over to his sons Stanley and Walter, and semiretired, although he kept his eye on the business until his death in the early forties. By the time Stanley and Walter took over, the farm contained about twenty-two acres, sixteen of which were under cultivation. Celery remained an important crop, but they also grew tomatoes, spinach, carrots, beets, radishes, Boston lettuce, and dandelions.

When James Alexander's sons took over, Walter went to market with whatever they had for sale. He left with the load near midnight, returned around nine in the morning, slept a while, and then went to work on the farm. Stanley was the early-to-rise farmer. My sister-in-law, Barbara Wilson Fuery, still lives next to the farm and reminisces about the days when her father and uncle ran the farm. "It was a relatively short season with really not a very good living earned by the two families. They worked very hard and were very frugal people." Of course, this period included not only the depression but also World War II.

As was customary on most farms, the children helped out as soon as they were old enough. Alan remembers being reprimanded, when he was a child, for handling the Boston lettuce roughly while he was packing it for market. Even today he talks about how he disliked washing and packing dandelion greens, which was one of their major crops. In 1945 he was paid ten cents an hour to work after school and on Saturdays. The boys were permitted to leave school during the fall to help with the harvest. For pocket money, Alan was allowed to cut lettuce that remained in the field after harvest and sell it house to house for five cents a head. His first retailing experience came when he was allowed to sell the strawberries his uncle Stanley grew. He set the berries on a plank by the side of Pleasant Street near the present location of the farm stand and sold them for twenty cents a quart. Donald not only sold eggs from his house but also had an egg route in Lexington and Arlington from the end of World War II until the year after the first stand was opened. Many of the first customers at the new stand were from Donald's egg route.

During this period when Stanley and Walter ran the farm, it was bounded on one side by a brook, and on the other by a hay field. A dairy farm adjoined the property, and another farm on the hill overlooked Wilson Farm. Lexington was a rural community. After World War II, the population of Lexington changed. One by one, the many farms were developed for houses. The town is now a suburb of Boston and a residential community. Of course, Wilson Farm has changed too — it is no longer a small market garden. The dairy farm next door has been developed with houses, and the farm on the hill is now conservation land.

Cousins Alan and Donald took over the business in 1953 and opened the first farm stand that year. Today the farm, which has been expanded from sixteen acres to over thirty, is as up to date as possible. There are fork lifts in the barnyard and conveyor belts in the packing house. Greenhouses and a garden shop have been added in Lexington and two hundred fifty acres of farmland in New Hampshire. Wilson Farm of New Hampshire, less than an hour from the Lexington farm, grows vegetables both for wholesale and for our farmstand. Donald's son Calvin helps manage the New Hampshire farm. There is also an Ayrshire dairy farm in Maine. Although we no longer have horses on the farm, we usually keep two Ayrshire heifers or a couple of piglets to show the children who visit. Alan, following the tradition set by his father, goes to market, while Donald is the farmer, as was his father. Donald's two boys are both involved in the farming part of the business, and Alan's and my children are busy with the retail section. We are truly a family farm, with wives and children pitching in to do any jobs that are necessary.

I did not grow up on a farm, so I never take it for granted. It is glorious to see the fields across from our house — the neat rows, bright greens, Ruby (red) lettuce, fields of flowers to cut and sell. We are unique, a touch of country in suburbia. It is certainly the best of both worlds. Boston is only thirty minutes away, and we have close neighbors, farm friends, and a hundred-year legacy of quality produce.

"Massachusetts Grown and Fresher" is the slogan of the Massachusetts Department of Agriculture, and I tried to keep it in mind as I was developing the cookbook. The recipes include the wonderful fruits, vegetables, and poultry grown at Wilson Farm and other local and New England farms. Although, in our area, most vegetables and fruits, shipped in from other states, Mexico, South America, Europe, and even as far away as New Zealand, are available year round, produce is always best when eaten fresh from the farm.

It is inspiring to have an unlimited supply of vegetables and fruits to work with when I am feeling creative (or hungry) and want to cook. I have been providing recipes as a customer service at our farm stand for over ten years, starting, quite frankly, because we overcropped with eggplant one fall. We weren't alone — every farm in the vicinity had too much. Alan said, "Help!" and we decided to set up double displays and offer recipes for eggplant. Our merchandising strategy worked so well that it wasn't long before I was asked to do the same for carrots and spinach. Soon I had a new job — creating and supplying recipes for our customers.

As much as I enjoy cooking, like most cooks I find that other matters often take precedence. Therefore, for the most part, my recipes are not time-consuming. I delight in making pies and desserts, but they are often prepared at the last minute. I have included many quick and simple dessert recipes that may be served warm. I find this is the best way to handle dessert for unexpected (or expected) company on a busy day.

I have found it exciting to introduce our farm crew to vegetables that many had never tried. Our customers have also sampled many of my dishes. Truthfully, cooking is most enjoyable when you share the results, which is probably why I have always loved to entertain. Writing and testing the recipes certainly gave me a wider audience than I ever had in my dining room. I hope to entice you, the readers of this book, to try some of the many tempting ways to use farm-fresh produce.

The Wilson Farm

Country Cookbook

Recipes from New England's
Favorite Farm Stand

1

Appetizers

The title Appetizers covers a variety of dishes. Within this chapter you will find recipes for dips and spreads for crackers or vegetables, hot and cold hors d'oeuvres, and first-course selections that have to be eaten at the table.

Fruit, except for juice, seemed too prosaic to include in the recipe section, although I often serve it as an appetizer. Fruit cups, plain or with sherbet, are always popular. I cut up whatever fruit I have available at least two hours before serving, add sugar, and chill. Even if the fruit is sweet, I sprinkle a tiny bit of sugar over it because the juice is so much better that way. Blueberries, peeled, sliced peaches, and cubed melon make an excellent combination. A mint leaf or two adds a cool flavor to this or other mixed fruit. I also serve melon, peeled and sliced or simply in unpeeled wedges, before meals with a slice of lime. Melon and prosciutto (or ham) are a great twosome. Cubes of melon, wrapped with prosciutto and secured with a toothpick, are lovely cold hors d'oeuvres that can be made ahead.

For a hot-fruit hors d'oeuvre, cut peeled pears (or peaches) into 1- to 2-inch pieces. Wrap each piece with a half slice of bacon, secure with a wooden toothpick, and broil, turning once, until the bacon is crisp. Anjou pears are particularly good cooked this way.

Raw vegetable (crudité) platters with dips are great any time, but especially for parties. Some people blanch the vegetables briefly (so they aren't quite crisp), then chill them before serving. I, personally, prefer the taste and texture of chilled raw vegetables so I never do this. I include not only the typical carrot and celery sticks, peppers, cherry tomatoes, scallions, broccoli, cauliflower, radishes, and cucumbers, but also turnips (particularly rutabaga), parsnips, summer squash and zucchini, kohlrabi, and mushrooms on my platters. When I fix platters for a party, I hollow out enough of a red or green cabbage to hold a small container for the dip. Red cabbages are often compact enough to hold the dip, but green ones are likely to leak. But even in red cabbage, it's safer to use a container. I also use cabbage leaves around the cabbage and dip to hold the vegetables, alternating red and green leaves and filling each leaf with a contrasting vegetable. The green cabbage leaves just pull off, but the red ones don't. Core the cabbage and place it, cored side down, in a large pot of boiling water. After it's been blanched for a few minutes, you should be able to pull off the leaves. Layer the leaves with paper towels (red cabbage gives off red coloring until dry) and chill before filling. I also use whole red or green cabbage to hold toothpicked, cold hors d'oeuvres or cubes of cheese or meat.

Several of the first-course appetizers may be served in larger portions as main courses — for instance, the quiches, crepes, and Crab au Gratin. And three of the main courses — Ziti with Vegetables, Stuffed Cabbage Rolls, and Stuffed Green Peppers (see Index for recipes) — could be used as appetizers.

❧ Basil Dip for Raw Vegetables

3 ounces cream cheese, softened
1½ cups sour cream
¼ pound medium sharp cheddar cheese, grated

1 tablespoon tomato paste
2 to 3 tablespoons chopped fresh basil

Blend the cream cheese, sour cream, cheddar cheese, and tomato paste in a food processor or blender until smooth. Stir in the basil and refrigerate for at least 2 hours before serving.

❧ Broccoli Dip

MAKES 3 TO 3½ CUPS

Serve this dip with crackers or raw vegetables. I like it spicy hot and use more than a dash of Tabasco sauce. However, at the farm, I found that people prefer sauce less hot, so I suggest that you start with a dash, then add more to your taste.

3 cups cooked, coarsely chopped broccoli
½ cup plain yogurt
¼ cup mayonnaise
3 ounces cream cheese, softened
1 tablespoon lemon juice

2 tablespoons minced onion
½ teaspoon minced garlic
¼ teaspoon salt
Dash Tabasco sauce (or to taste)

Steam the broccoli (or blanch it in boiling water). Drain well and chop. Place all the ingredients in a food processor or blender. Blend until the ingredients are well mixed but not puréed. Chill before serving.

❧ Dill-Tofu Dip for Raw Vegetables

MAKES 2 CUPS

We sell tofu (bean curd) at our farm stand. A staple in the Orient, it has only recently become popular in the States. It is nutritious, high in protein, and very adaptable. Since it has little flavor of its own, it picks up flavors from the other ingredients in a recipe. I use this dip for raw vegetables, but it is also good as a salad dressing.

1 cup sour cream
8 ounces hard or soft tofu
1/4 teaspoon garlic powder (or 1 small clove garlic, minced)
2 teaspoons finely minced onion

1/3 teaspoon salt
Pepper to taste
2 tablespoons chopped fresh dill

Place all the ingredients, except the dill, in a food processor or blender. Blend them until smooth. Stir in the chopped dill and refrigerate for at least 2 hours before serving.

NOTE: This dip may be made with other fresh herbs.

❧ Eggplant Dip

MAKES APPROXIMATELY 2½ CUPS

Preheat the oven to 400°F.

1½ pounds eggplant
⅓ cup mayonnaise
2 hard-boiled eggs
¼ cup minced parsley
¼ cup minced onion
2 cloves garlic, peeled and minced

3 tablespoons oil
2 tablespoons lemon juice
½ teaspoon salt
⅛ teaspoon pepper

Prick a large eggplant with a fork several times. Put it on a cookie sheet and bake at 400°F for 35 to 40 minutes or until very soft. Remove it from the oven, cut in half, and drain, cut side down, in a colander until almost cool. Scoop the eggplant from the skin (about 2 cups) and purée in a blender or food processor with all the remaining ingredients (it doesn't have to be perfectly smooth). Chill. Correct the seasoning and serve with crackers.

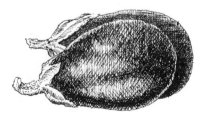

♨ Guacamole (Avocado) Dip

This is a chunky dip. I use a potato masher to get the right texture. It isn't spicy, so if you want hot, spicy guacamole, stir in more chili powder, a dash of Tabasco sauce, or a pinch of cayenne pepper.

3 *ripe avocados (about 2 pounds)*

1 *tablespoon minced onion*

1 *tablespoon lime juice*

¾ *teaspoon salt (or to taste)*

⅛ *teaspoon ground pepper*

1 *tablespoon mayonnaise plus additional to cover dip*

½ *teaspoon chili powder (or to taste)*

Dash garlic powder (or ⅛ teaspoon minced garlic)

¾ to 1 *cup peeled, seeded, and coarsely chopped tomatoes*

Peel the avocados and place them in a large mixing bowl. Add the onion, lime juice, salt, pepper, 1 tablespoon mayonnaise, chili powder, and garlic powder. Mash these ingredients together until well mixed. Stir in the tomato. Correct the seasoning and chill. To prevent discoloration, cover the dip with a thin layer of mayonnaise, which can be stirred in just before serving.

NOTE: Instead of the usual crackers or nachos, serve guacamole with slices of zucchini or summer squash or pieces of red or green pepper as dippers.

ᴥ Sherried Cheese Ball

All the ingredients should be at room temperature before you start to make this cheese ball.

8 ounces medium sharp cheddar
  cheese, grated
8 ounces cream cheese, softened
2 ounces blue cheese
3 tablespoons butter, softened
1 teaspoon Worcestershire sauce

1 teaspoon dry mustard
1/4 teaspoon garlic powder
1 to 2 tablespoons sherry (or to
  taste)
1/2 cup chopped fresh parsley

Blend all the ingredients, except the parsley, in a large bowl with an electric mixer or food processor. When smooth, chill until firm. Form into a ball and roll in chopped parsley. Serve with crackers.

ᴥ Chicken Liver Spread (Paté)

2 eggs, hard-boiled
8 slices bacon, crisply cooked
  and crumbled
1/2 cup butter or margarine
1 pound chicken livers, drained
1 cup chopped onions
1 small clove garlic, minced
1/2 teaspoon salt

1/8 teaspoon freshly ground
  pepper
1/2 teaspoon Worcestershire sauce
1 tablespoon sherry (optional)
  Chopped red onion
  (optional)

Hard-boil the eggs, chop, and set aside. Cook the bacon, crumble, and set aside. Melt the butter in a large frying pan. Add the chicken livers, onions, and garlic and cook over medium heat until the onions are tender and the livers almost done (about 5 minutes). Do not overcook the livers. Place the contents of the frying pan, including the drippings, in a large mixing bowl or food processor and add the eggs, bacon, salt, pepper, Worcestershire, and sherry. Beat or blend until fairly smooth. Chill. Top with chopped red onion before serving. Serve with crackers or toast rounds.

ᨌ Stuffed Cucumber Sandwiches

MAKES ABOUT 36 SANDWICHES

These are fancy small tea sandwiches. The cucumbers are hollowed out (cored), filled with cream cheese and dill, chilled, and then thinly sliced. The slices are placed on bread rounds and are ready to serve. They may be made ahead, covered, and refrigerated until serving time.

2 6-inch cucumbers or 1 long
    (10-inch) burpless cucumber
3 ounces cream cheese
1 tablespoon butter, softened
    Dash garlic powder

1 to 1½ tablespoons finely
    chopped dill
12 to 18 slices soft bread
    Mayonnaise

Remove the ends from the cucumbers. Peel, if desired. Cut them in half crosswise. (Cut the burpless into three pieces.) Remove the seeds from the cucumbers with a knife or apple corer.

Mix the cream cheese, butter, garlic powder, and dill. Stuff the cucumbers with this mixture. Chill for at least 3 hours before slicing.

Cut 1½- to 2-inch rounds out of the soft bread. Spread each round lightly with mayonnaise. Cut the stuffed cucumbers with a very sharp knife into ⅛- to ¼-inch slices. Top each bread round with a slice of stuffed cucumber. Serve chilled.

NOTE: Very finely chopped radishes may be used in place of dill. Zucchini may also be stuffed and used for sandwiches.

❧ Lettuce and Chipped Beef Tidbits

MAKES ABOUT 30 HORS D'OEUVRES

These bite-sized cold hors d'oeuvres have a chipped (or smoked) beef filling surrounded with lettuce that's anchored with a toothpick. The secret is to use only enough lettuce to fold around the filling once.

1 package (2½ ounces) cooked chipped beef
1 tablespoon butter
¼ teaspoon minced garlic
4 ounces cream cheese, softened
½ teaspoon lemon juice

1 tablespoon mayonnaise
2 teaspoons chopped parsley
8 leaves Boston lettuce, washed and dried

Chop the beef into small pieces. Melt the butter in a small frying pan over medium heat and add the chopped beef. Sauté the beef for 1 to 2 minutes. Add the garlic and sauté for 1 minute longer. Don't brown the garlic. Mix the hot beef, garlic, and remaining ingredients, with the exception of the lettuce, in a mixing bowl. Place in the refrigerator to chill for at least 1 hour. When firm, place bite-sized portions (1 teaspoon) of beef filling on small pieces of lettuce (about 3 inches square). Fold or roll the sides and ends of the lettuce pieces in to cover the filling. Secure with toothpicks. Cover with a damp dishtowel and refrigerate if not serving immediately.

≈ Deviled Eggs

MAKES 12 DEVILED EGGS

These eggs are not spicy. Add some cayenne pepper or a dash of Tabasco sauce if you feel they are too mild.

6 large eggs, hard-boiled and cooled (see note)
1/4 cup mayonnaise
1/4 to 1/2 teaspoon dry mustard
1/8 teaspoon salt
Dash pepper, freshly ground

1/8 teaspoon Worcestershire sauce
1 tablespoon chopped parsley (optional)
Dash cayenne pepper, or more to taste (optional)
Olive slices (optional)

Peel the eggs and slice them in half lengthwise. Carefully remove the egg yolks and put them into a mixing bowl with the mayonnaise, mustard, salt, pepper, Worcestershire sauce, chopped parsley, and cayenne pepper. Mix all the ingredients with a fork or spoon until smooth. Stuff the egg whites with the mixture and top with a slice of olive. Chill before serving.

NOTE: There are many ways to hard-cook eggs. Put a single layer of large eggs in a saucepan, cover with cold water to 1 inch over the eggs, cover the pan, and bring the water to a boil. Remove the pan from the heat and let the eggs sit in the hot water, covered, for about 16 minutes (large eggs). After 16 minutes, drain the hot water from the eggs and run cold water over them until they are cool. To make deviled eggs, bring the eggs to a simmer, covered, then remove the cover and simmer for about 12 minutes, stirring several times at the beginning of the simmer, to keep the yolks centered. Remove the pan from the heat, drain the water, and cover the eggs with cold water. Let them cool completely.

♨ Asparagus Roll-Ups

Roll-ups are a good springtime hot hors d'oeuvre. They are simply asparagus stalks with bread rolled around them — difficult to describe, but delicious to eat. They can be put together early in the day and baked just before serving. How many you make is up to you. One spear of asparagus and one slice of bread make two hors d'oeuvres, so it's simple to plan whether to make four for yourself or fifty for a party.

Preheat the oven to 425°F.

6 spears asparagus
6 slices soft bread, white or dark
1 tablespoon butter, softened
1 tablespoon butter, melted
1 teaspoon mustard

6 slices ham, cooked and thinly sliced, or
6 slices Swiss cheese, thinly sliced

Trim the asparagus and cook until tender. Drain well and set aside.

Remove the crusts from the bread. White bread is best because its flavor doesn't overpower the asparagus. *Important:* Roll each slice of bread with a rolling pin until flat and thin.

Spread each slice of flattened bread lightly on one side with softened butter and a little mustard. Place a thin slice of ham or Swiss cheese on one half of the slice of bread.

Top the ham or cheese with a spear of asparagus and roll up as tightly as possible, starting on the ham-covered side and making sure the edge is sealed by the butter. Cut each roll in half.

Place the rolls, sealed side down, on a cookie sheet. Brush the tops (both bread and exposed asparagus) with melted butter. Bake at 425°F for approximately 15 minutes or until brown. Serve warm.

✿ Deep-Fat-Fried Cauliflower with Horseradish Dipping Sauce

This batter may be used for other vegetables as well as cauliflower. Broccoli should be blanched, but sliced onion rings and small mushrooms can be coated and fried raw.

1 medium head cauliflower in florets

BATTER

1 egg
1 cup milk
1 cup flour
1 teaspoon baking powder
1 teaspoon salt
3 tablespoons oil
  Oil for deep frying

DIPPING SAUCE

⅓ cup mayonnaise
¼ cup light cream
1 tablespoon grated horseradish
⅛ teaspoon coarsely ground pepper

Steam the cauliflower florets (or blanch them in boiling, salted water) until almost tender. Drain and set aside to cool and let dry.

Beat together the egg, milk, flour, baking powder, salt, and 3 table-spoons oil until smooth. When you're ready to fry, heat the oil in a deep-fat fryer or a deep saucepan. Coat the cauliflower with batter and fry a few at a time in the hot oil.

Mix the dipping sauce ingredients. Serve the cauliflower with the sauce on the side.

ꙮ Cauliflower and Red Pepper Puffs

MAKES 12 PUFFS

Preheat the oven to 400°F.

12 toast rounds
1 cup cooked chopped
   cauliflower
¼ cup diced red pepper, ¼-inch
   pieces
1 tablespoon butter
4 ounces cream cheese,
   softened

⅛ teaspoon salt
Dash pepper
Dash Tabasco sauce (more for
   spicier taste)

Cut 1½- to 2-inch rounds from soft white sandwich bread with a
cutter or glass. Place them on a cookie sheet and toast them for
approximately 5 minutes at 400°F or until lightly browned. Remove from the oven and set aside.

Blanch or steam 1½ cups cauliflower florets. When soft, drain and
chop. Measure 1 cup.

Melt the butter in a small frying pan, add the red pepper, and
sauté until it softens. Stir in the cauliflower and sauté for 1 minute.
Remove from the heat.

Place the cream cheese in a mixing bowl. Stir in the warm cauliflower and pepper. Add the salt, pepper, and Tabasco sauce to
taste. Mound the cauliflower mixture on the toast rounds and bake
at 400°F for about 10 minutes or until they begin to brown. Serve
warm.

❧ Stuffed Mushrooms

Tomato adds a different touch to an old favorite. These may be made ahead and cooked just before serving — a necessity for hot hors d'oeuvres. They use quite a bit of butter, but, frankly, that's what makes them taste so good!

Preheat the oven to 350°F.

3 slices bacon	¹/₂ cup peeled, seeded, finely chopped tomato
18 to 24 mushrooms (1¹/₂ to 2 inches in diameter)	²/₃ cup dry bread crumbs
5 tablespoons butter	Salt and pepper to taste
¹/₃ cup finely chopped onion	1 tablespoon grated Parmesan cheese
1 small clove garlic, finely minced	

Cook the bacon until crisp, crumble, and set aside. Remove and set aside the stems from the mushrooms.

Melt 1 tablespoon of the butter and brush it on the mushroom caps. Place the mushroom caps on a cookie sheet and make the filling.

Trim the mushroom stems and chop them coarsely. You need 1 to 1¹/₄ cups. Melt 3 tablespoons of the butter in a large frying pan. Add the chopped mushroom stems and the onion. Sauté until they soften. Add the garlic, tomato, and remaining 1 tablespoon butter. Sauté only until the tomato and garlic are heated through (about 1 minute). Remove from the heat and add the bread crumbs, bacon, salt and pepper, and cheese. Mix very well.

Fill the mushroom caps and bake at 350°F for 15 to 20 minutes or until the mushrooms are cooked. Serve warm.

❧ Small Stuffed Potatoes or Mini Twice-Baked Potatoes

These may be put together early in the day and cooked just before serving, which makes them good party fare. I have included two sets of ingredients for stuffing, so you have a choice (or make two sets of potatoes for a large group).

Preheat the oven to 400°F.

6 small (new) potatoes, 1½ inches in diameter

Butter, softened, to grease potatoes

Stuffing No. 1

1 tablespoon butter or margarine
⅓ cup sour cream
1 sweet Italian sausage, cooked

¼ teaspoon salt
Freshly ground pepper to taste

Wash the potatoes and grease them lightly with the softened butter. Prick them with a fork and bake at 400°F for approximately 35 minutes or until soft.

When they are cool enough to handle, cut them in two and scoop out part of the potato pulp into a bowl, being careful not to damage the skins. Beat the potato with an electric mixer until smooth. Heat the butter and sour cream slightly in a small saucepan, then beat it into the potato. Cut the sausage into very small pieces and stir it into the potato mixture. Add the salt and pepper. Spoon the potato mixture into the skins. Bake at 400°F for about 15 minutes and serve.

Stuffing No. 2

2 tablespoons butter or margarine

1 tablespoon finely minced onion

2 tablespoons light cream

¼ teaspoon salt

Freshly ground pepper to taste

⅓ cup lightly packed shredded medium sharp cheddar cheese

2 slices bacon, crisply cooked and crumbled (optional)

Wash the potatoes and grease them lightly with the softened butter. Prick them with a fork and bake at 400°F for approximately 35 minutes or until soft.

When they are cool enough to handle, cut them in two and scoop out part of the potato pulp into a bowl, being careful not to damage the skins. Beat the potato with an electric mixer until smooth.

Heat the butter in a small frying pan. Add the onion and sauté until it softens. Stir in the cream and heat slightly. Add the butter, onion and cream mixture, and salt and pepper to the potato. Beat in until well mixed. Stir in the cheese and bacon. Spoon the potato mixture into the skins. Bake at 400°F for about 15 minutes or until the cheese melts.

♨ Potato Skins

Potato Skins are very popular, and with good reason. They are simple to make and taste great. I leave quite a bit of potato in mine, and save what I scoop out to use in other ways.

Preheat the oven to 400°F.

8 small to medium baking potatoes

⅓ cup butter or margarine, melted

Salt

2 cups sour cream

10 slices bacon, crisply cooked and crumbled

1 to 2 tablespoons finely chopped onion

Scrub the potatoes, prick them with a fork, and bake at 400°F for approximately one hour or until done. Refrigerate or let sit until they are cool enough to handle.

Cut the potatoes into sixths (cut them in half lengthwise, then each piece into three pieces), and scoop out some of the potato. Brush the potato skins with melted butter on all sides. Sprinkle the insides with salt and place on a cookie sheet, skin side down. Potatoes may be refrigerated at this point for later baking. Bake at 400°F for about 10 minutes.

While the potatoes are baking, mix the sour cream, bacon, and onion. Remove the potato skins from the oven and top each with a spoonful of the sour cream mixture before serving.

NOTE: I sometimes top the potato skins with bacon and Swiss cheese. To do this, you need slices of cooked bacon and thin squares of cheese. Bake the buttered potato skins at 400°F for 5 to 8 minutes. Remove them from the oven and place ⅛ piece of cooked bacon on each, covering the bacon with a square of cheese. Return to the oven and continue baking until the cheese melts.

◐ Spicy Curried Squash Balls

I developed these out of necessity when I was asked to make hors d'oeuvres from Massachusetts-grown vegetables for an early March party. Needless to say, except for greenhouse vegetables, no vegetables are harvested at that time, as our fields may still be snow-covered. Since a great deal of butternut squash is grown (and stored to sell during the winter months) in our state, this was an acceptable vegetable. Somehow, squash pie doesn't go very well with cocktails, so I served these bite-sized tidbits for curry lovers.

Preheat the oven to 400°F. Grease a cookie sheet.

3 tablespoons butter or
    margarine
1/4 cup finely chopped onion
1 1/2 cups peeled, uncooked, and
    grated butternut squash
1/2 cup bread crumbs

1 egg, slightly beaten
1/4 teaspoon salt
1 teaspoon curry powder
1/8 teaspoon cayenne pepper

Melt the butter in a small frying pan. Add the onions and sauté until soft but not brown. Place the onion and butter in a mixing bowl and add the remaining ingredients. Mix thoroughly. Form the mixture into bite-sized balls (a little smaller than a cherry tomato). Place on a greased cookie sheet. Bake in the upper third of the oven at 400°F for about 15 minutes or until lightly brown. Turn once after 5 minutes. Serve hot on toothpicks.

These are a bit like stuffing balls but they are very spicy. Vary the amounts of curry and cayenne to suit your personal taste.

NOTE: Grate the raw squash on the small or medium hole of a grater.

🌿 *Rumaki (Chicken Livers Wrapped with Bacon)*

MAKES APPROXIMATELY 24

I love chicken livers but many people don't. Surprisingly, I find that when I cut the livers into small pieces and wrap them with a little more bacon than I normally use, even the teenage boys who work for us think they're terrific.

½ pound chicken livers
⅓ cup soy sauce
½ teaspoon grated ginger root (optional)
12 slices bacon (approximately)

Sliced water chestnuts
Scallions trimmed to 3 inches (optional)
Wooden toothpicks

Cut the chicken livers into two or three pieces. Put them into a small mixing bowl with the soy sauce and ginger. Stir to coat and marinate for at least 2 hours.

Cut the bacon slices in half. Place a piece of chicken liver on each piece of bacon, and add a slice of water chestnut and a trimmed scallion. Wrap the bacon around all and secure with a toothpick. Place on a broiler pan and broil for approximately 5 minutes on each side, turning once, until the bacon is crisp. Serve warm.

✿ Barbecued Chicken Wings

MAKES 16 PIECES

Barbecued wings are good but messy, so make sure you have plenty of napkins handy.

Preheat the oven to 400°F.

8 small chicken wings (about
   1½ pounds)
½ cup chopped onion
1 tablespoon cider vinegar
1 tablespoon lemon juice
2 tablespoons dark brown
   sugar
⅓ cup catsup

1 teaspoon Worcestershire sauce
¾ teaspoon dry mustard
¼ teaspoon salt
¼ cup water
   Tabasco sauce to taste

Remove the tips from the chicken wings and discard. Separate the other pieces, trimming off any excess fatty skin, if necessary. You will have sixteen little wing sections. Place the pieces on a shallow pan (or cookie sheet) and bake at 400°F for 15 minutes.

While the pieces are cooking, mix the remaining ingredients, adding as much Tabasco sauce as you desire.

Remove the wings from the oven and transfer them to a shallow 2-quart baking dish. Pour the sauce over the wings and return them to the oven, uncovered. Bake at 400°F for 20 minutes longer, spooning the sauce over the chicken and turning often. Serve warm.

ꙮ Chicken Swedish Meatballs

These hors d'oeuvres are similar to those made with beef and pork. Use either a meat grinder or a food processor to grind up the raw chicken.

MEATBALLS

4 chicken breasts, 2 to 2½
  pounds, skinned and boned
  (see page 187)
2 tablespoons butter
⅓ cup finely minced onion
2 eggs, beaten
1¼ cups dry bread crumbs
1 tablespoon chopped parsley

1 teaspoon salt
⅛ teaspoon pepper
½ cup milk
½ teaspoon poultry seasoning
¼ cup oil

Grind the chicken breasts. You will have 2 to 2½ cups ground chicken. Place the chicken in a large mixing bowl.

Melt the butter in a small frying pan. Add the onion and sauté until soft. Add the onion and butter to the chicken together with the beaten eggs, crumbs, parsley, salt, pepper, milk, and poultry seasoning. Mix very well. Roll into small balls the size of cherry tomatoes. Heat the oil in a large frying pan over medium-high and brown the meatballs. Remove the meatballs from the pan but reserve the oil.

SAUCE

¼ cup flour
2 cups hot water
1 teaspoon Worcestershire sauce

½ teaspoon salt
Pinch cayenne pepper
¾ cup sour cream

Stir the flour into the oil remaining in the frying pan. Place the pan over medium heat and stir in the hot water, Worcestershire sauce, salt, and cayenne pepper. Cook until smooth and thick. Stir in the sour cream.

Return the meatballs to the pan. Cook over medium-low heat for about 20 minutes before serving. Serve in a chafing dish with toothpicks on the side.

NOTE: The meatballs are also fine as a main course with egg noodles or rice.

❧ Hot Stuffed Celery

I thought it would be fun to serve hot stuffed celery instead of cold as an appetizer. These are filled with a tomato stuffing rather than cream cheese and served with a light cheese sauce. One or two pieces of stuffed celery topped with sauce is probably enough for an appetizer, except for someone who has a very large appetite.

> 8 3- to 4-inch pieces celery
>   (large end)
> 1¼ cups chicken broth

Wash and cut the celery, using the large end (those pieces hold more stuffing), and save the rest for another use. Place the chicken broth in a frying pan, bring to a simmer, and add the celery pieces. Poach the celery for about 6 to 8 minutes or until it softens a bit. Remove the celery and set aside, reserving the chicken broth.

NOTE: The celery should not be overcooked. It has to remain somewhat firm to hold the stuffing.

Preheat the oven to 350°F.

STUFFING

> 3 tablespoons butter or
>   margarine
> 2 tablespoons minced onion
> ¼ cup finely chopped green
>   pepper
> ½ cup peeled, seeded, chopped
>   tomato
> 2 teaspoons chopped fresh basil
>   (½ teaspoon dried)

> ¼ teaspoon salt
>   Pepper
> ¾ cup dry bread crumbs
> 1 tablespoon grated Parmesan
>   cheese

Melt the butter in a medium frying pan. Add the minced onion and chopped green pepper and sauté until soft. Add the tomato, basil, salt, and pepper and stir until hot but not cooked (less than 1 minute). Add the bread crumbs and Parmesan cheese. Mix thoroughly, then add enough chicken broth to moisten. Fill the celery with the stuffing and place it in a shallow 1½-quart baking dish (about 6½ by 10 inches). Pour ⅓ cup of the chicken broth into the bottom of the dish and bake, uncovered, at 350°F for 30 minutes.

Prepare the sauce while the celery is baking.

CHEESE SAUCE

2 tablespoons butter or margarine
2 tablespoons flour
½ cup chicken broth
½ cup light cream
½ teaspoon salt

⅛ teaspoon freshly ground pepper
¾ cup shredded Longhorn (Colby) cheddar cheese

Melt the butter in a 2-quart saucepan. Stir in the flour and cook until bubbly. Stir in the broth and cream and cook, stirring, until the broth thickens and boils. Add the salt, pepper, and cheese, and cook until the cheese melts.

Serve the celery topped with cheese sauce on individual plates.

ᴣᴱ Crepes with Chicken and Asparagus or Broccoli

Betty Wilson avoided me while I was writing this book because I was always looking for volunteers to test recipes, and she was watching her weight. However, when I tested these, I invited her to lunch and served them to her. They got her approval (and she cleaned her plate!). Use either asparagus or broccoli. This is a good recipe for using leftover turkey.

CREPES

2 eggs	¼ teaspoon salt
1 cup milk	2 tablespoons butter, melted
1 cup flour	

Beat all the crepe ingredients together and refrigerate for 1 to 2 hours. When ready to cook the crepes, lightly oil a small 5- to 6-inch frying pan or crepe pan. Heat it over medium-high. Place approximately 3 tablespoons of the batter in the hot pan. Rotate the pan so the bottom is covered. Cook the crepe for about 1 minute and turn. Cook it for about 1 more minute and remove from the pan. Stack the crepes between sheets of waxed paper. Crepes may be prepared in advance and kept covered until ready to fill.

When ready to assemble crepes, preheat oven to 375°F.

FILLING

2 cups chopped 1-inch pieces
    broccoli or ½- to 1-inch
    pieces asparagus
6 tablespoons butter or
    margarine
1½ cups sliced mushrooms
3 tablespoons chopped
    shallots
6 tablespoons flour
1½ cups chicken broth

1½ cups light cream
1 teaspoon salt
¼ teaspoon ground pepper
2 cups cooked chicken (or
    turkey)
1 to 2 tablespoons grated
    Parmesan cheese

Steam or blanch the asparagus or broccoli until barely tender.
Drain well and set aside.

Melt the butter in a 3-quart saucepan. Add the mushrooms and
shallots and sauté until soft. Put in the flour and stir until mixed.
Add the broth and light cream and cook, stirring, until the sauce
thickens. Stir in salt and pepper to taste.

Mix about one-third of the sauce with the chicken and broccoli.
Fill the crepes with this mixture and place them, seam side down,
in a large, shallow dish (or two smaller ones). Pour the remaining
sauce over the crepes and sprinkle with the Parmesan cheese.
Bake at 375°F for 15 to 20 minutes or until the sauce is bubbly.
Place the crepes briefly under the broiler to brown, if desired.

NOTE: For added flavor, stir 2 to 3 tablespoons of sherry into the
sauce.

♨ Crab au Gratin in Green Pepper Boats

SERVES 8

Serve this rich appetizer, with a knife and fork, before a simple meal. Allow one filled pepper boat per serving.

Preheat the oven to 375°F.

$^1\!/_2$ to $^3\!/_4$ pound cooked crabmeat
    4 small green peppers
    1 cup small pieces seeded zucchini
    3 tablespoons butter or margarine
    1 tablespoon minced onion
  $^1\!/_3$ cup $^1\!/_4$-inch diced red pepper
    3 tablespoons flour

$^3\!/_4$ cup light cream
$^1\!/_2$ cup milk (or more, if necessary)
$^1\!/_2$ teaspoon salt
$^1\!/_8$ teaspoon ground pepper
$^1\!/_2$ cup lightly packed shredded Swiss cheese
  2 tablespoons grated Parmesan cheese

Break up the crabmeat, if necessary. Cut the peppers in half, stem to blossom end, making boats or shells. Remove the seeds and blanch the pepper halves in boiling water for 5 minutes. Drain and set aside while preparing the gratin sauce.

Cut a small zucchini into quarters, lengthwise. Remove most of the seeds and cut it into $^1\!/_4$- to $^1\!/_2$-inch pieces. Set aside.

Melt the butter in a 2-quart saucepan. Add the onion, zucchini, and red pepper, and sauté until slightly soft. Stir in the flour. Add the cream and milk and cook, stirring, until thick. Stir in the salt, pepper, and Swiss cheese. Mix the crabmeat into the sauce. Fill the pepper boats three-quarters full with the crab mixture and sprinkle the tops with Parmesan cheese. Place as flat as possible in a shallow baking dish. Bake at 375°F for 15 to 20 minutes or until lightly brown and slightly puffy. Serve hot.

NOTE: This dish may also be cooked in scallop shells or individual ramekins. If you do not use green pepper shells, increase the amount of diced red pepper to $^1\!/_2$ cup. If you desire, stir in 2 to 3 tablespoons of sherry with the Swiss cheese.

❧ Asparagus and Ham Quiche

SERVES 8

The quality of the ham makes a difference in the taste of the quiche, so be sure to use the best available.

Prepare a 9-inch shell (recipe, page 228). Either bake it partially at 375°F for about 8 minutes or brush the inside with slightly beaten egg white to prevent a soggy bottom.

Preheat the oven to 375°F.

2 cups trimmed, ¼-inch slices asparagus
1 cup cooked ham in ¼-inch cubes (about ⅓ pound)
1 cup lightly packed shredded Swiss cheese
1 tablespoon finely minced onion

3 eggs
1⅓ cups light cream
½ teaspoon salt
⅛ teaspoon pepper

Steam the asparagus (or blanch in boiling water) for 5 minutes. Drain very well and let cool slightly.

When the asparagus is slightly cool, place it in a mixing bowl. Add the ham, cheese, and onion and stir gently. Place the mixture in the pie shell. Beat the eggs, cream, salt, and pepper together with a wire whisk or eggbeater and pour over the asparagus mixture in the pie shell. Bake at 375°F for 40 to 45 minutes or until set. Test by inserting a knife; when it comes out clean, the quiche is done.

NOTE: Cut the asparagus on a diagonal to get attractive ovals. Leave the tips whole.

ℒ Broccoli Quiche

SERVES 8

You can always add a little cooked bacon, ham, or sausage if you don't like a meatless quiche.

Prepare a 9-inch pie shell (recipe, page 228). Either bake it partially at 375°F for about 8 minutes or brush the inside with slightly beaten egg white to prevent a soggy bottom.

Preheat the oven to 350°F.

2 eggs
1 egg yolk
¾ cup milk
¾ cup light cream
½ teaspoon salt
½ teaspoon dry mustard
⅛ teaspoon pepper
1 teaspoon Worcestershire sauce

Dash nutmeg
Dash cayenne pepper
1½ cups cooked, chopped broccoli
1 cup lightly packed shredded Swiss cheese

Beat the eggs, egg yolk, milk, cream, salt, mustard, pepper, Worcestershire, nutmeg, and cayenne together in a large mixing bowl until well blended. Spread the broccoli and cheese over the bottom of the pie shell. Pour the liquid mixture over the broccoli and cheese. Bake at 350°F for approximately 40 minutes or until lightly brown and set.

ℒ Spinach Strudel

MAKES 24 TO 36 PIECES

This recipe isn't difficult to prepare but it does take some time. It produces three strudels and, depending on how you slice them, up to 36 hors d'oeuvres. It's simple enough to make one-third of the recipe for only one strudel. These are also good served as a first course. First, defrost a package of frozen phyllo (sometimes spelled filo) leaves as directed on the package. You have to plan ahead to make this recipe because the phyllo requires overnight defrosting in the refrigerator.

Preheat the oven to 375°F.

15 defrosted strudel leaves (phyllo)

2 pounds fresh, untrimmed spinach (1½ pounds trimmed)

13 tablespoons butter or margarine

1 cup chopped onion

1 cup thinly sliced scallions

½ cup chopped, fresh dill (1 tablespoon dried)

5 eggs

1 pound feta cheese, broken into small pieces

¼ cup dry bread crumbs

Trim and wash the spinach. Place the wet leaves in a large pot and cook over medium heat until the spinach wilts. You should not have to add more water. Drain, squeeze as dry as possible with your hands, and chop. You need 1½ cups of chopped spinach.

Melt 5 tablespoons of the butter in a large frying pan. Add the onions and scallions and sauté over medium heat until soft. Add the spinach and dill and cook, stirring, for 2 to 3 minutes. Remove from the heat.

Beat the eggs in a large mixing bowl. Add the feta cheese and mix well. Stir in the spinach mixture.

Make the three strudels as follows: Melt the remaining 8 table-spoons (½ cup) of butter. Using 5 phyllo leaves for each strudel, brush each leaf with melted butter, sprinkle with ½ to 1 teaspoon bread crumbs, and stack until you have a stack of 5 leaves. Spread one-third of the spinach mixture along the long edge of the stack. Fold in the ends and roll as a jelly roll, the long way. Place the strudel, seam side down, on a cookie sheet and brush the top with melted butter. Make two more strudels in this fashion. Bake at 375°F for approximately 45 minutes. Slice and serve warm.

🔥 Spinach Custard or Quiche

SERVES 8

Quiche is not as popular as it used to be. However, this one tastes too good to abandon. I cook it in an 8-inch-square pan, cut it into squares, and serve it as a vegetable or a first course without a crust. It is also the right amount for a 9-inch quiche if you want to make a pastry crust.

Either prepare a 9-inch pie crust (recipe, page 228) and brush the inside with slightly beaten egg white or butter an 8-inch-square pan.

Preheat the oven to 350°F.

$1^{1}/_{2}$ *pounds fresh, untrimmed spinach (1 pound trimmed)*
$^{1}/_{2}$ *pound bacon (or $^{3}/_{4}$ cup cooked, chopped ham)*
4 *eggs*
1 *cup light cream*
$^{1}/_{3}$ *cup milk*

$^{1}/_{2}$ *teaspoon salt*
$^{1}/_{8}$ *teaspoon cayenne pepper*
2 *teaspoons finely minced onion*
1 *cup lightly packed shredded Swiss cheese*

Wash and trim the spinach. Place the wet leaves in a large pot and cook over medium heat until the spinach wilts. You should not have to add more water. Drain, squeeze as dry as possible with your hands, and chop. You should have about 1 cup of chopped spinach.

Cook the bacon until crisp and crumble. Set aside. Beat the eggs, cream, milk, salt, and cayenne pepper together in a large mixing bowl with an eggbeater or wire whisk. Stir the onion, cheese, chopped spinach, and bacon into the egg mixture and mix very well. Fill the pie shell or buttered casserole with the spinach mixture. Bake at 350°F for 40 to 45 minutes or until the custard puffs and a knife inserted in the center comes out clean.

✒ *Hot Spiced Cranberry Juice*

SERVES ABOUT 12

Have you ever made cranberry juice? As he was drinking some, a guest asked if I had squeezed the cranberries. No, I hadn't squeezed them, but I had cooked them.

> 6 cups cranberries
> 6 cups water
> 1½ to 2 cups sugar
>
> 1 whole cinnamon stick
> 4 whole cloves

Place all the ingredients in a 4-quart saucepan. Cover, bring to a boil, uncover, and cook for about 10 minutes or until the cranberries burst and are very soft. Strain into another container, pressing the liquid from the berries as you strain. Serve warm or chilled.

NOTE: When the juice chills, it thickens to a consistency similar to that of apricot nectar. It may be thinned down slightly with water, if you desire. For the holidays, serve chilled cranberry juice with a spoonful of sherbet on top. Lime sherbet is particularly pretty at Christmas.

✒ *Hot Mulled Cider*

SERVES ABOUT 12

We serve this drink at the farmstand when the weather gets cold. Of course, our customers enjoy it, but the farm crew, who are outside selling Christmas trees, really appreciate it.

> ½ gallon apple cider
> 1 small orange, quartered
> 12 whole cloves
>
> 12 whole allspice
> 1½ cinnamon sticks
> 1 to 2 tablespoons sugar

Place all the ingredients in a large pot. If you don't want to strain the cider, tie the cloves, allspice, and ½ stick cinnamon in cheesecloth. Leave the whole cinnamon stick loose. Cover. Bring the mixture to a boil, lower the heat, and simmer for at least 30 minutes or until the flavors are blended. Serve warm.

NOTE: Add wine, rum, or other liquor if you desire. The cider is also good chilled.

2

Soups

*P*eople at *Wilson Farm* like soup. Both the customers and the employees were willing to taste test any soup that I made. I tested most of these soups during the cold weather, when they were always welcome. Surprisingly, I never lacked for volunteers to taste hot soup, even during the summer months.

When I serve food or do demonstrations at the farm, quick-cooking soups receive the most interest (after the dessert recipes, naturally). I make fresh Spinach Soup quite often. During October, I serve Cream of Pumpkin Soup, as well as other soups and cooked vegetables, in a heated pumpkin shell. (See the directions for cooking with pumpkin shells in the vegetable chapter on page 174.)

Several of the soups included in this chapter, such as Chilled Strawberry Soup, may be served cold. They provide a great start to a meal on a hot day. It is important to remember to check the seasoning in soups after they have been chilled. Chilling diminishes the flavors, and you may have to add more salt or other spices.

In most of the cream soups, I have tried to use potato or rice, rather than flour, as a thickener. I usually think of cream soups as appetizers. However, they are good luncheon dishes when accompanied by a salad and rolls or muffins. Some of the other soups are hearty enough to be served as a main course. You could certainly invite guests to a Sunday night supper of Chicken and Vegetable Soup, a green salad, bread or muffins, and dessert.

Any herb may be used to change the flavor of soups. I have not used many, as I prefer the taste of the vegetables. However, a touch of mint in the Cream of Carrot Soup (especially if it is to be chilled) adds a bit of interest, and dill in Cream of Parsnip Soup is also good. Use your favorite herbs in small amounts to get the desired hint of flavor.

You will find recipes for Chicken and Beef Broth. I make Chicken Broth from fowl (see page 40) and use the meat to make many dishes. I usually have Chicken Broth in my freezer, but Beef Broth is another story. I don't use it as often, so I make it only as needed. I confess that when I'm in a hurry, I use the full-strength canned broth that doesn't have to be diluted. I find it is an adequate, if not ideal, substitute.

🌹 Beef Broth

When you don't have time to stand over your stockpot while the meat and bones brown, you may brown them at 350°F for 45 to 60 minutes.

2 shin bones with meat (2½ to 3 pounds total)	¼ teaspoon whole peppercorns
10 cups water	2 bay leaves
3 stalks celery	½ teaspoon dried thyme (2 teaspoons fresh)
1 large yellow onion, sliced	1 cup unpeeled, unseeded chopped tomato
⅓ cup coarsely chopped parsley	3 teaspoons salt
1 large, unpeeled carrot, cut into 1-inch pieces	
4 whole cloves	

Cut the meat from the bones into 1-inch pieces.

Heat an 8-quart soup pot and add the bones and meat. If the bones contain marrow, scrape it out and use it to brown the meat. Enough fat should cook out of the meat to make browning easy. If not, add a tablespoon of oil. When the meat and bones are very well browned (the browner the meat, the darker the broth), add the water and bring it to a boil. Skim the broth if necessary. Add the remaining ingredients and lower the heat. Simmer, covered, for about 3 hours, skimming as necessary. Remove from the heat and strain. If you want a concentrated flavor, return the broth to stove and simmer, uncovered, until the broth is slightly reduced (about 30 minutes). Refrigerate. Remove the fat from the surface before using the broth.

NOTE: I discard the vegetables but save the meat, which I use to make hash, add to soup, or simply serve plain.

🌹 Chicken Broth

I make Chicken Broth often because I like to use the chicken meat from fowl (see page 187) for many dishes (for example, salad, tetrazzini, mornay). You can freeze the necks and backs from chickens you cook for other purposes until you have 5 to 6 pounds and use them to make broth. Chicken Broth may also be frozen, so you can keep a supply on hand at all times.

1 5- to 6-pound cut-up fowl (stewing chicken)	1 large, unpeeled carrot, cut into ½-inch chunks
2 stalks celery, cut into 3-inch pieces (use the leaves)	⅓ cup parsley leaves (flat leaf, if available)
1 large yellow onion, sliced	½ teaspoon dried thyme (1 to 2 teaspoons fresh)
1 bay leaf	2 teaspoons salt
6 to 10 peppercorns	8 to 10 cups cold water

Wash the chicken and place it in a large, heavy 8-quart soup pot. Add the remaining ingredients, using enough water to cover, and bring to a boil over high heat. Lower the heat and simmer, covered, for 3 hours for fowl, 2 hours for fryers, skimming the top if necessary. Remove chicken, cut the meat from the bones, and save for another use. Strain the broth, discard the vegetables, and refrigerate. When the broth is chilled, remove the fat from the top before using it.

Note: If necessary, this broth may be made with a 3½ pound fryer, but will not be as flavorful.

❧Escarole-Chicken Soup

SERVES 8

This soup is very simple to prepare once the chicken is cooked and the escarole washed and chopped. Cook the chicken as explained in the recipe for chicken broth (page 40). When it is done, remove the chicken from the bones and strain the broth. You need both broth and chicken. Any additional chicken beyond 2 cups, save for another use (chicken salad sandwiches?). I hesitate to mention it, but canned tomatoes work just as well as fresh in this soup as long as they are well drained. Of course, fresh ones are better, especially during the summer, when fresh, ripe tomatoes are available.

8 cups Chicken Broth (recipe, page 40)

2 cups small pieces cooked chicken

12 cups chopped escarole (about 1½ pounds)

⅔ cup chopped scallion

⅓ cup small macaroni (like Mini-Mac)

2 cups peeled, seeded, and chopped tomatoes

½ to 1 teaspoon salt

Freshly ground pepper to taste

Grated Parmesan or Romano cheese

Prepare the chicken broth. Remove the meat from the bones, cut up 2 cups of chicken, and set aside.

Wash and slice (or chop coarsely) 1½ pounds of escarole. Heat the chicken broth in a large, 6-quart soup pot. When the broth starts to boil, add the scallions and macaroni. Reduce the heat and simmer, covered, for 10 to 15 minutes or until the macaroni is almost cooked. Add the tomatoes, chicken, escarole, salt, and pepper. Return to a boil, lower the heat, and simmer, uncovered, for 5 to 10 minutes longer or until the escarole is tender. Top with grated Parmesan or Romano cheese just before serving.

🌺 Spinach Soup

Spinach Soup is very easy to make and really tastes good. Even our non-spinach-eating son eats it. Serve the soup as soon as the spinach is done, so the bright green color isn't lost. The spinach should be added just before serving. Don't cover the pot or the spinach will darken, and although the flavor will still be good, the color won't.

10 cups washed, stemmed, and coarsely chopped raw spinach (1 to 1½ pounds untrimmed)	1 small clove garlic, finely chopped
1½ tablespoons butter or margarine	6 cups Chicken Broth (recipe, page 40)
½ cup thinly sliced scallions or chopped onion	½ cup uncooked small pasta or rice
½ cup peeled, finely chopped carrots	Salt and pepper to taste
	Grated Parmesan cheese (optional)

Prepare the spinach.

Melt the butter in a 4-quart saucepan. Add the scallions, carrots, and garlic and sauté until the scallions begin to soften (2 to 3 minutes). Add the chicken broth. Cover and bring to a boil, then add the pasta or rice. Simmer, covered, until the pasta or rice is cooked (5 to 15 minutes). Just before serving time, stir the spinach into the hot broth mixture. Cook, uncovered, for 2 to 3 minutes or until the spinach wilts. Add salt and pepper to taste. Top with grated Parmesan cheese.

🌹 Quick and Easy Cabbage and Sausage Soup

Overcooking causes this soup to lose its attractive color. If you have to start it a while before serving, it's better to cook the leeks and add the broth, but don't add the other vegetables or sausage until almost serving time. From that point, it takes less than 10 minutes to cook. Also, don't make the mistake of using Italian sausages with fennel seed, as I once did. The anise flavor overpowered the soup. Plain sweet Italian sausages are best.

4 to 6 *sweet Italian sausages, cooked*
   1 *tablespoon butter or margarine*
   ¾ *cup chopped leeks*
   3 *cups Chicken Broth (recipe, page 40)*
   3 *cups Beef Broth (recipe, page 39)*
   8 *cups coarsely chopped cabbage*

1 to 2 *tablespoons chopped fresh basil (1 teaspoon dried)*
   1½ *cups peeled, seeded, and chopped tomatoes*
   1 *clove garlic, peeled and minced*
      Salt and pepper to taste

Cook the sausages and cut them into small pieces or slice very thinly. Set aside.

Melt the butter in a 4-quart pan and add the chopped leeks. Sauté over medium heat until soft, then add the chicken broth and the beef broth. Cover and bring to a boil. Stir in the cabbage, basil, tomatoes, and garlic. Cover, return to a boil, lower the heat, and uncover. Simmer, uncovered, for 3 to 5 minutes and add the sausage. Simmer for 2 to 3 minutes longer, uncovered, until the cabbage is crisp-tender. Add salt and pepper and serve immediately.

❧ Onion Soup

SERVES 6 TO 8

I certainly didn't lack for volunteer tasters when I was working on this recipe. I think the wonderful onion smell in my kitchen must have drifted across the street to the farm, since the whole crew seemed to be waiting for me when I arrived with samples. I use regular yellow onions, but sweet, Spanish ones are also nice (and don't take as long to slice!). Naturally, the soup tastes better with homemade Beef Broth (recipe, page 39).

3 tablespoons butter
2 tablespoons oil
3 pounds yellow onions, peeled and thinly sliced
1 teaspoon sugar
6 cups Beef Broth
1 teaspoon Worcestershire sauce

1 bay leaf
1 clove of garlic
½ teaspoon salt
¼ cup dry sherry
Grated Parmesan cheese

Heat the butter and oil in a heavy 6-quart pot. Add the onions and stir to coat. Sprinkle the sugar over the onions and cook, uncovered, over medium-low heat, stirring occasionally, until the onions are soft and transparent — about 15 to 20 minutes. Raise the heat to medium and cook the onions, stirring often, until they darken in color to gold or pale brown — about 20 minutes. Be very careful not to burn the onions. Add the broth, Worcestershire, bay leaf, garlic, and salt. Cover, raise the heat, and bring to a boil. Lower the heat and simmer for 20 minutes. Remove the bay leaf and garlic, stir in the sherry, sprinkle with cheese, and the soup is ready to serve. To serve Baked Onion Soup, continue with the following recipe.

🌸 Baked Onion Soup

You need six to eight ovenproof bowls, depending on their size. The directions for making toasted French bread rounds (croûtes) are below. If you prefer, you can serve the *croûtes* on top of the soup without adding the cheese topping. Or you can simply top the soup with Croutons (recipe, page 117).

Preheat the oven to 400°F.

Onion Soup (recipe opposite)

CROÛTES

*6 to 8 slices (¹/₄- to ¹/₂-inch thick) French bread
Butter, softened*
¹/₂ cup grated Parmesan cheese

2 cups shredded Gruyère or Swiss cheese

Spread one side of each slice of French bread with butter, then sprinkle heavily with grated Parmesan cheese. Bake at 400°F for about 10 minutes or until brown.

Mix the shredded cheese and ¼ cup grated Parmesan cheese. Spoon the Onion Soup into ovenproof bowls. Top each with a toasted bread round and then a layer of the cheese mixture. Bake at 400°F for 10 to 15 minutes or until the cheese melts. Place the bowls under the broiler to brown the cheese, if desired.

❧ Chilled Cucumber and Watercress Soup

For an elegant lunch on a hot summer day, serve this soup topped with a bit of chopped mint. If you prefer, serve it hot, topped with chopped parsley or dill.

3 tablespoons butter or margarine

$1/3$ cup chopped yellow onion

$2/3$ cup peeled, chopped potato

4 to 5 cups unpeeled, chopped cucumbers (2 large — $3/4$ pound each)

$1/2$ cup lightly packed watercress leaves

2 cups Chicken Broth (recipe, page 40)

1 cup heavy cream
Salt and pepper to taste
Chopped fresh mint (optional)

Melt the butter in a large frying pan, and add the onion, potato, cucumbers, and watercress. Sauté the vegetables for 3 to 5 minutes or until they are slightly wilted. Remove them from the heat and place them in a 3-quart saucepan. Add the chicken broth, then bring to a boil. Lower the heat and simmer for 15 minutes or until all the vegetables are soft. Remove from the heat and purée in a blender or food processor until very smooth. Add the cream and salt and pepper. Chill. Correct the seasoning before serving. Top each serving with mint.

Chilled Fresh Strawberry Soup

SERVES 4 TO 6

This slightly tart soup has a beautiful pink color. Don't panic if you don't get out all the seeds when you strain the soup. It just proves that you used fresh strawberries.

1 quart strawberries, washed and hulled	⅔ cup heavy cream
1½ cups water	⅛ teaspoon salt (or to taste)
½ cup sugar	Dash cinnamon
1 tablespoon cornstarch	½ cup sour cream (optional)

Combine the strawberries, water, and sugar in a 3-quart saucepan. Cover and bring the water to a boil. Lower the heat, remove the cover, and simmer, uncovered, until the berries are very soft — about 15 minutes. Purée the mixture in a blender or food processor, then strain it through a sieve or cheesecloth to remove the majority of the seeds. Return it to the pan. Stir the cornstarch, cream, salt, and cinnamon together in a small mixing bowl. Stir the cream mixture into the strawberry mixture and heat until the soup begins to simmer. Simmer for 1 to 2 minutes or until slightly thick. Remove from the heat and chill for at least 2 hours. Top each serving with a small spoonful of sour cream.

🌺 Cream of Asparagus Soup

SERVES 8

1 tablespoon butter or
  margarine
1/3 cup chopped scallions
1/2 cup chopped celery
2 cups Chicken Broth (recipe,
  page 40)
2 cups water
1 cup diced (1/2-inch pieces)
  potato (1 medium)

4 to 41/2 cups 1/2-inch pieces
  asparagus (green only,
  about 2 pounds,
  untrimmed)
1/2 teaspoon salt
1/8 teaspoon pepper
  (preferably white)
1 cup light cream (less to
  taste)

Melt the butter in a 3- or 4-quart saucepot over medium-low heat.
Add the scallions and celery and sauté for 3 to 4 minutes. Add the
broth, water, potato, asparagus, salt, and pepper. Bring to a boil,
lower the heat and simmer, covered, for 15 to 20 minutes or until
the potato and asparagus are very tender. Purée in small batches in
a blender or food processor. Return to the pan and stir in the
cream. Correct the seasoning and heat gently before serving.

🌺 Cream of Cauliflower and Leek Soup

SERVES 6 TO 8

2 tablespoons butter or
  margarine
11/2 cups sliced leeks (well
  washed, white part only)
3 cups Chicken Broth (recipe,
  page 40)
1 pound cauliflower, washed
  and divided into pieces

1/2 teaspoon salt
1/2 to 1 cup light cream
  Salt and pepper to taste
  Chopped parsley or dill
  (optional)

Melt the butter in a 4-quart saucepan. Add the leeks and sauté
until they are soft but not brown. Add the broth, cauliflower, and
salt. Cover the pan, bring the broth to a boil, lower the heat, and
simmer, covered, for 6 to 8 minutes or until the cauliflower is soft.
Purée in small batches in a blender or food processor. Return to
the pan and stir in the cream. Add salt and pepper. Heat gently
and top with parsley or dill.

🌺Cream of Broccoli Soup

SERVES 8

3 to 4 cups cooked, chopped
    broccoli
  2 cups broccoli cooking
    water
  2 cups Chicken Broth
    (recipe, page 40)
  $\frac{1}{2}$ cup coarsely chopped
    celery

$\frac{1}{3}$ cup coarsely chopped onion
$\frac{1}{3}$ cup lightly packed parsley
$\frac{1}{3}$ cup uncooked rice
$\frac{1}{3}$ teaspoon salt
$\frac{1}{2}$ cup light cream
$\frac{1}{4}$ cup milk (more if necessary)

Wash and trim about 1½ pounds of broccoli. Divide the large
pieces and cook in boiling, salted water until tender (about 6 to 8
minutes). Drain the broccoli well, reserving 2 cups of the cooking
water. Chop the broccoli coarsely and set aside. You should have
3 to 4 cups of chopped broccoli.

Pour the broth and cooking water into a 4-quart pot. Bring to a
boil and add the celery, onion, parsley, rice, and salt. Return to a
boil, lower the heat, and simmer for about 20 minutes or until the
rice is very soft. Add 3 cups of the broccoli and simmer for 5
minutes longer. It will be very thick. Remove from the heat. Purée
in small batches in a blender or food processor. Return the purée
to the pan and stir in the cream, milk, and ½ to 1 cup additional
broccoli, if desired. Correct the seasoning and heat gently.

NOTE: For a typical cream soup, don't add the extra broccoli.
However, I think the soup is more interesting with the added texture of the unpuréed broccoli.

🌺 Cream of Carrot Soup

SERVES 6 TO 8

Curry powder gives the soup a special taste. I use one teaspoon, but the amount is a matter of taste.

2 tablespoons butter
1/2 cup chopped onions
3 cups peeled, sliced carrots (1 to 1 1/4 pounds without tops)
3/4 cup peeled, diced potato
1/2 cup sliced celery
3 cups Chicken Broth (recipe, page 40)

1/2 teaspoon salt
Freshly ground pepper, to taste
1 cup light cream
1 teaspoon curry powder, or to taste (optional)

Melt the butter in a 4-quart pan. Add the onions and sauté until soft. Add the carrots, potato, celery, broth, salt, and pepper. Cover, bring to a boil, lower the heat, and simmer, covered, for 15 to 20 minutes or until the vegetables are very tender. Purée in small batches in a blender or food processor, or press through a sieve. Return to the heat and stir in the cream. Correct the seasoning and heat gently before serving. This soup may also be chilled. Correct the seasoning after chilling.

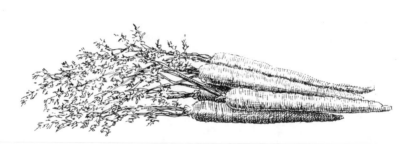

🌹Cream of Mushroom Soup

SERVES 6 TO 8

Cream of Mushroom is one of my favorites. It is a little more time-consuming to prepare than most of my recipes, but it is well worth the effort.

6 tablespoons butter
1 pound mushrooms, trimmed and cut into large slices (4 to 5 cups)
3 cups Chicken Broth (recipe, page 40)
²/₃ cup chopped celery

¹/₃ cup chopped onion
3 tablespoons flour
1¹/₃ cups milk
  Salt and pepper to taste
¹/₂ cup heavy cream (optional)

Melt 3 tablespoons of the butter in a 4-quart saucepan. Add the mushrooms and cook over medium heat until soft — about 3 minutes. Add the broth, celery, and onion and simmer for 20 to 30 minutes or until the vegetables are very tender.

Purée in a food processor or blender or press through a sieve and set it aside while you make a cream sauce, as follows:

Melt the remaining 3 tablespoons of butter in a 3-quart saucepan. Stir in the flour and cook for 1 minute. Remove the pan from the heat and slowly stir in the milk. Return the pan to the heat and cook, stirring, until the sauce comes to a boil. Continue cooking for 1 minute longer, stirring. Remove the sauce from the heat and stir in the mushroom purée. Add salt and pepper. Heat gently. Do not boil. Before serving, whip the cream and top each bowl with a heaping spoonful of unsweetened whipped cream.

NOTE: When possible, use older, darker mushrooms for this soup because their flavor is stronger than that of the prettier white ones.

✿ Cream of Leek and Potato Soup

SERVES 8

Wash the leeks thoroughly before you start, because sandy soup isn't very appetizing. This soup, whether hot or cold (vichyssoise), is *so* delicious. I'm probably in the minority, but I like it better hot.

3 tablespoons butter or margarine

6 cups sliced leeks (5 to 6, white part only)

¾ cup coarsely chopped onion

4 cups peeled, ½-inch-diced white potatoes

4 cups Chicken Broth (recipe, page 40)

1 teaspoon salt

1½ cups heavy cream

⅛ teaspoon ground white pepper (optional)

Chopped chives (optional)

Melt the butter in a 4-quart pot. Add the leeks and onion and cook for about 5 minutes or until they are wilted but not brown. Add the potatoes, broth, and salt and bring to a boil. Lower the heat and simmer, covered, for 20 to 30 minutes or until the vegetables are very tender. Purée in small batches in a blender or food processor, or press through a sieve. Return the purée to the pan, and stir in the cream and pepper. Add salt if necessary. Heat gently and sprinkle with chopped chives. This soup may be chilled, but check the seasoning just before serving.

🌸 Cream of Parsnip Soup

SERVES 6 TO 8

2 tablespoons butter
¾ cup chopped leeks
3 cups peeled, sliced parsnips
½ cup sliced celery
¾ cup peeled, diced potato

4 cups Chicken Broth (recipe,
  page 40)
½ teaspoon salt
  Freshly ground pepper to taste
1 cup light cream

Melt the butter in a 4-quart pan. Add the leeks and sauté until soft.
Add the parsnips, celery, potato, broth, salt, and pepper. Cover,
bring to a boil, lower the heat, and simmer, covered, for 15 to 20
minutes or until the vegetables are very tender. Purée in small
batches in a blender or food processor or press through a sieve.
Return to the heat and stir in the cream. Correct the seasoning
and heat gently before serving.

❧ Cream of Pumpkin or Squash Soup

SERVES 8

It's fun to serve this soup in a pumpkin shell for a holiday dinner or on a buffet table. The color is lovely whether you use pumpkin or winter squash.

2 tablespoons butter
1 cup coarsely chopped leeks
5 to 6 cups peeled, ½-inch-diced pumpkin or winter squash (about 1½ pounds)
4 cups Chicken Broth (recipe, page 40)

⅓ cup uncooked rice
1 to 1½ cups light cream (or a combination of milk and cream)
Salt and pepper to taste

Melt the butter in a 4-quart pot. Add the leeks and sauté for 3 to 4 minutes or until soft. Add the pumpkin, broth, and rice. Bring to a boil, lower the heat, and simmer, covered, until the rice and pumpkin are done. It takes about 20 minutes, but be sure the rice is done, or it won't purée smoothly. Purée in small batches in a blender or food processor. Return to the pan and stir in the cream. Season to taste. Heat gently (do not boil) before serving.

NOTE: For a variation, flavor the soup with a small amount of sugar and a dash of cinnamon *or* add ½ teaspoon or more of curry powder to serve Curried Pumpkin Soup.

🌸 Cream of Squash or Pumpkin and Apple Soup

SERVES 8

It took me a number of tries to get the proportions that suit my fancy. I didn't want either the apple or the squash to predominate. The good-natured gang at the farm kept sampling and sampling. The recipe is what I finally settled on. You can use any winter squash or pumpkin and any apple that isn't too tart. I used only a little ground nutmeg, but if you like spicy soup, add a touch of cinnamon.

2 tablespoons butter or margarine
1/3 cup onion chopped
2/3 cup chopped celery
3 cups peeled, 1/2-inch cubes squash or pumpkin
2 pounds apples, peeled, cored, and thickly sliced (4 to 5 apples)
3 cups Chicken Broth (recipe, page 40)

1 cup water
1/4 cup uncooked rice
1 cup light cream
1/4 teaspoon salt
2 teaspoons sugar (or to taste)
1/4 teaspoon nutmeg

Melt the butter in a 4-quart saucepan. Add the onion and celery and sauté until soft. Add the squash, apples, broth, water, and rice. Cover and bring to a boil. Lower the heat and simmer covered, for about 20 minutes or until the rice and squash are done. Remove from the heat and purée in small batches. Return to the pan and stir in the cream, salt, sugar, and nutmeg. Heat gently. Don't boil. Sprinkle nutmeg over each serving.

NOTE: This soup can also be chilled. If you chill it, correct the seasoning before serving.

✿ Cream of Tomato Soup

SERVES 6

There is no comparison between canned and fresh tomatoes, so make this soup during the summer when ripe, local tomatoes are plentiful.

2 *cups Chicken Broth (recipe,*
page 40)
4 *cups peeled, seeded, chopped*
ripe tomatoes
1/3 *cup coarsely chopped onion*
1/2 *cup coarsely chopped celery*

1/4 *cup uncooked rice*
1/2 *teaspoon sugar*
1/2 *to 1 cup light cream or milk,*
heated
Chopped fresh herbs or
croutons

Place the broth, tomatoes, onion, celery, rice, and sugar in a 3-quart saucepan. Cover, bring to a boil, lower the heat, and simmer for 25 to 30 minutes or until the vegetables are very soft and the rice is done. Purée the mixture in small batches in a blender or food processor or press through a sieve. Return the mixture to the pan and stir in the hot cream or milk. Correct the seasoning. Add more sugar or salt if necessary. Heat gently. Do not boil.

Serve hot, topped with croutons or chopped fresh dill, basil, or tarragon. Or serve chilled, topped with one of the herbs or with crisply cooked, crumbled bacon.

NOTE: The amount of cream or milk required depends on the flavor of the tomatoes. If they are very flavorful, you can use more cream.

✿ Split Pea Soup

SERVES 8

I made Split Pea Soup several times during the winter and put the pot out so customers could help themselves. The soup always disappeared instantly. It is not necessary to add linguica, especially if you use a ham bone with considerable meat. However, linguica makes an even heartier soup and proved extremely popular around the farm.

1 pound yellow split peas,
 soaked overnight
9 cups water
1½ cups chopped onion
1 clove garlic, chopped
1 bay leaf
2 teaspoons salt
2 ham hocks (¾ pound total)
 or ham bone

1 cup peeled, diced carrot
½ cup diced celery
1 pound precooked linguica or
 kielbasa, cut into ½-inch
 pieces (optional)

Rinse and pick over the split peas. Soak them in 6 cups of water overnight in a large soup pot.

The next day, add 3 cups of water, the onion, garlic, bay leaf, salt, and ham hocks to the soaked peas. Bring to a boil, lower the heat and simmer, covered, for 1 hour. Skim as needed. Add the carrot and celery and cook for 45 minutes longer. Stir in the linguica and cook for 15 minutes longer. Remove the ham hocks and correct the seasoning.

🌺 Zucchini and Cheddar Cheese Soup

SERVES 6 TO 8

If you use light-colored cheese (not orange Longhorn or Colby cheddar), you will get a pretty green soup. I use medium sharp rather than sharp cheese, so as not to obscure the zucchini flavor. You can also make the soup with broccoli or cauliflower.

2½ cups Chicken Broth (recipe, page 40)
¼ cup chopped onion
⅓ cup chopped celery
5 cups unpeeled, sliced zucchini (about 1½ pounds)
½ teaspoon salt
⅛ teaspoon pepper

2 tablespoons butter or margarine
2 tablespoons flour
½ cup light cream or milk
1 cup, lightly packed, grated medium sharp cheddar cheese (¼ pound)

Place 2 cups of the broth, the onion, celery, zucchini, salt, and pepper in a 3- or 4-quart saucepan. Cover and bring to a boil. Lower the heat and simmer, covered, for 20 to 25 minutes or until very soft. (The zucchini skin has to cook.) Purée this mixture in small batches in a blender or food processor and set aside.

Make the cheese sauce as follows: Melt the butter in a 2-quart saucepan and add the flour. Cook, stirring, for 1 minute. Remove from the heat and stir in the remaining ½ cup of broth and the cream. Return to the heat and cook, stirring, until the mixture thickens and comes to a boil. Remove from the heat and stir in the cheese. When the cheese melts, stir the sauce into the puréed vegetables. Correct the seasoning. Heat gently. Do not boil. Add more milk or cream if the soup is too thick.

🌺Corn Chowder

SERVES 8

A bowl of Corn Chowder tastes especially good on rainy summer days. Be sure that the corn you use is mature. When I serve corn on the cob, I choose young, small-kerneled corn. However, for corn chowder, mature, heavier corn offers more flavor.

$1/3$ cup $1/4$-inch cubes salt pork
$1/2$ cup peeled, chopped onion
$1/4$ cup chopped green pepper
$1 1/2$ cups hot water
$1 1/2$ cups peeled, cubed potatoes
  3 cups corn kernels, cut from fresh corn ears

$1/2$ teaspoon salt
$1/8$ teaspoon pepper
  2 cups milk
  1 cup light cream

Cook the salt pork in a 4-quart pot until crisp. Add the onion and pepper and cook them with the salt pork until soft. Remove the salt pork and vegetables from the pan with a slotted spoon and drain the fat from the pan. Return the salt pork and vegetables to the pan and add the hot water, potatoes, corn, salt, and pepper. Bring this mixture to a simmer and cook, covered, for 10 to 15 minutes or until the potatoes are tender. Add the milk, cream, and additional seasoning, if necessary. Heat the chowder but do not boil. When the chowder is very hot, remove it from the heat and let it sit for 30 minutes to improve the flavor. Reheat and serve.

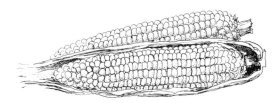

🌺 Parsnip Chowder

This chowder is very popular at the farm and with our customers. The bacon complements the sweet parsnip flavor.

4 slices bacon
1 cup coarsely chopped onion
3 cups peeled, $^1/_4$- to $^1/_3$-inch cubes parsnips
1 cup peeled, $^1/_4$- to $^1/_3$-inch cubes potatoes
1 cup peeled, $^1/_4$- to $^1/_3$-inch cubes carrots
2 cups water

1$^1/_2$ teaspoons salt
$^1/_4$ teaspoon freshly ground pepper
1 tablespoon butter or margarine
1$^1/_2$ cups milk
1 cup light cream

Cook the bacon until very crisp. Set it aside, reserving 2 tablespoons of the bacon fat. Put the fat in a 4- to 6-quart pan, add the onion, and sauté over medium-low heat until soft but not brown. Add the parsnips, potatoes, carrots, water, salt, and pepper. Cover and bring to a boil. Lower the heat and simmer for about 10 minutes or until the vegetables are tender. Stir in the butter, milk, and cream. Break the reserved bacon into small pieces and add them. Correct the seasoning and heat gently but don't boil.

❦ Summer Minestrone with Shell Beans

SERVES 8

Kidney beans are a basic ingredient in minestrone. However shell beans make an excellent substitute when they are available during the summer. Our daughter, who always orders minestrone when it is on the menu, had me make it several times before she was satisfied with the results. (Of course, it could be that she just wanted it for lunch more than once!)

2 slices bacon, diced (or 1½ tablespoons oil)

¾ cup coarsely chopped onion

6 cups Beef Broth (recipe, page 39)

1 tablespoon tomato paste

1 clove garlic, minced (1 to 1½ teaspoons)

2 cups fresh shell beans, shelled

1 bay leaf

¾ cup ½-inch pieces green beans

½ cup peeled, ¼-inch diced carrots

½ cup sliced celery

¾ cup peeled, ½-inch diced potatoes

2 cups ½-inch diced zucchini pieces

1½ cups peeled, seeded, chopped tomatoes

2 teaspoons chopped basil or ½ teaspoon dried (or more to taste)

1 tablespoon chopped parsley (preferably Italian flat leaf)

2 cups chopped cabbage or escarole

½ cup small-shell pasta (or elbow macaroni)

Salt and pepper to taste

Grated Parmesan or Romano cheese

Cook the bacon in a 6-quart pot until a little fat cooks out, or heat the oil. Add the onion and sauté until soft. Add the broth, tomato paste, garlic, shell beans, and bay leaf. Bring to a boil, lower the heat, and simmer, covered, for 40 minutes or until the beans are very soft. Remove the bay leaf and add the green beans, carrots, celery, potatoes, zucchini, tomatoes, basil, and parsley. Return to a boil and stir in the cabbage or escarole and pasta. Lower the heat and simmer, covered, for 20 minutes longer. Add salt and pepper. Serve with grated Parmesan or Romano cheese on the side.

NOTE: This minestrone is filling enough to serve at dinnertime as a main course with a salad and bread.

🌺 Hearty Chicken-Vegetable Soup

SERVES 8 TO 10

This recipe produces a very thick, and therefore filling, soup —
almost a stew. It certainly could be served on a cool night as a
main course with salad and bread. I always cook a fowl (stewing
chicken weighing 5 to 6 pounds) because I feel it makes the most
flavorful soup. However, the soup may be made with a frying
chicken. Pick out the largest one available (3 to 4 pounds). It
really doesn't matter whether the chicken is cut up or whole, but
I think it is easier to remove the meat from the bones if the
chicken is in pieces. It is time-consuming to make this soup, but
you can cook your chicken early in the day and finish the soup
just before serving. Once the broth is made and the chicken cut
up, it takes only about 30 minutes to finish the soup.

BROTH

> 1 *chicken*
> 2 *teaspoons salt*
> 2 *large stalks celery, cut
> into 2-inch pieces*
> 1 *large yellow onion,
> sliced*
> 8 to 10 *cups water (enough to
> cover chicken)*

SOUP

> ⅔ *cup uncooked small
> pasta (Mini-Mac or
> alphabets)*

> 2 *cups peeled, sliced
> carrots (rounds)*
> 1½ *cups green beans cut in
> ½-inch pieces*
> 1½ *cups celery cut into ¼-
> inch slices*
> 1 *cup chopped onion, in
> small pieces*
> 4 *cups coarsely chopped
> cabbage*
> 1½ to 2 *tablespoons chopped
> fresh basil (2 teaspoons
> dried) or other herbs to
> taste*
> *Salt and pepper to taste*

Remove the giblets and neck from the chicken and wash the
chicken. Combine the chicken, salt, celery, onion, and water in a
large (6- to 8-quart) soup pot. Bring to a boil, lower the heat, and
simmer, covered, for 3 hours for fowl or 2 hours for a frying
chicken. Skim the fat from the top while cooking, if necessary.
Remove from the heat, remove the chicken from the bones, and
cut it into small pieces when cool enough to handle. Set the
chicken aside. Discard the celery from the broth. Skim the fat from
the broth and strain it, if desired. It is not essential to strain the
broth, as the remaining onion will not harm the quality of the

soup. Bring the broth back to a boil and add the pasta, carrots, beans, celery, onion, and chicken pieces. Reduce the heat and simmer, covered, for 15 to 20 minutes or until the vegetables are tender. Stir in the cabbage and basil. Cook for 5 minutes longer or until the cabbage is crisp-tender. Correct the seasoning.

❀ Vegetable-Beef Soup

SERVES 8

Like the Hearty Chicken-Vegetable, the Vegetable-Beef is a very hearty soup. I serve this at the farm, using a heated pumpkin shell (see page 174) as a soup tureen. It is always a hit, both for the contents and the container.

1½ *pounds lean stew meat*
  2 *cups Beef Broth (recipe, page 39)*
  6 *cups water*
  1 *medium onion (¼ pound), coarsely chopped*
  2 *cloves garlic, peeled*
  1 *teaspoon salt*
⅛ *teaspoon ground pepper*
  1 *large bay leaf (or 2 small)*
  1 *medium onion, sliced*
¾ *cup sliced celery*
  1 *cup peeled, ¼- to ½-inch diced white or yellow turnip*
  1 *cup peeled, diced potatoes*

  1 *cup peeled, diced carrots*
¾ *cup ½-inch pieces green beans*
1½ to 2 *cups peeled, chopped tomatoes (seeded, if desired)*
  2 *tablespoons tomato paste*
  1 *teaspoon salt*
½ *teaspoon dried basil (2 teaspoons fresh)*
⅔ *cup uncooked small macaroni (like Mini-Mac)*

Trim the stew meat and cut it into small pieces. Place the meat, broth, water, chopped onion, garlic, 1 teaspoon salt, pepper, and bay leaf in a 6-quart pot. Bring to a boil, lower the heat, and simmer, covered, for 1 to 1½ hours. Remove the garlic and bay leaf. Add the sliced onion, celery, turnip, potatoes, carrots, beans, tomatoes, tomato paste, additional 1 teaspoon salt, and basil. Return to a boil, lower the heat, and simmer, covered, for 20 minutes. Stir in the macaroni and simmer for 15 to 20 minutes longer or until the vegetables and macaroni are tender. Correct the seasoning.

3

Quick Breads

Quick breads delight me because they totally suit my rather disorganized lifestyle. I'd rather have muffins than rolls, and I'd eat hot muffins for breakfast, lunch, and dinner and pancakes or waffles at any opportunity. When I'm having guests, I often make two or three kinds of fruit (or vegetable) loaves the day before entertaining. These loaves improve in flavor if wrapped and not sliced for twenty-four hours after they are made. I then offer a basket with a selection of quick breads. It's so much easier than trying to serve hot rolls.

Muffins aren't just for breakfast at our house. They are a nice addition to lunch when you serve a salad, soup, or other light dish. The wonderful thing about muffins is that you usually have the ingredients on hand when you have unexpected company, and muffins take only about twenty minutes to bake. Since I'm so fond of muffins, I usually make large ones, filling the pans three-quarters full. I must confess that I find the nonstick pans a blessing. Since muffins are such a last-minute item, I certainly don't want to be aggravated by muffins that stick.

Quick coffee cakes are also simple to make. They are a nice weekend morning treat. Our farm stand is open (and busy) on weekends, so I tend to serve breakfast breads on Tuesdays, when we're closed and have more time to sit around with a second cup of coffee.

Scott and I are the pancake lovers in our house. If I ask him what he'd like for breakfast on his day off, he always requests pancakes. I cooked butternut squash pancakes and served them at our stand one Sunday afternoon with our own honey from the New Hampshire farm. There was no way I could keep up with the demand. There must be many pancake lovers in the world, as every customer wanted to taste one. Like our customers, our employees enjoyed their roles as tasters for this chapter. One day I made apple bread three ways. Another day it was cranberry bread. Both times I lined up the loaves on a large bread board, and left a knife and a piece of paper asking the bread connoisseurs to comment on their choices.

These recipes are for breads that are made with locally grown vegetables and fruits. I particularly like to use cranberries and rhubarb, but the season is short, so I try to keep some in my freezer. Cranberries may be frozen whole and are a great deal easier to chop in a food processor than defrosted ones; when defrosted, they tend to be soft. My mother, who has been freezing rhubarb for many years, claims that adding a tiny bit of sugar to the rhubarb helps to retain the flavor. Of course, you still have to add sugar when you cook with it. I also keep some one-cup containers of cooked winter squash and pumpkin in the freezer for bread or muffins. When you cook squash or pumpkin, it is no bother to cook a little extra and freeze it for future use. It doesn't take long for one cup to defrost, and the bread or muffins taste better than those made with canned vegetables.

Apple Muffins

Substitute apple cider for the milk in these muffins to get added flavor. I put a little streusel mixture on the top, but that is an option.

Preheat the oven to 400°F. Grease a muffin pan for 8 large or 12 medium muffins.

MUFFINS

1 1/2 cups flour
 2/3 cup sugar
  2 teaspoons baking powder
 1/2 teaspoon salt
  1 teaspoon cinnamon
 1/4 teaspoon nutmeg
 1/4 cup butter or margarine, softened
  1 egg

 1/2 cup milk or apple cider
  1 cup peeled and finely chopped or coarsely grated apple (1 medium)

Sift the flour, sugar, baking powder, salt, cinnamon, and nutmeg into a large mixing bowl. Add the butter, egg, and milk or cider, and cut them in with a pastry blender or two knives until barely mixed — just long enough to moisten the dry ingredients. Stir in the apple. Spoon into the prepared pan. Top with streusel, if desired. Bake at 400°F for 20 to 25 minutes or until done.

STREUSEL MIXTURE (OPTIONAL)

 1 tablespoon butter, softened
 2 tablespoons flour
 2 tablespoons dark brown sugar

 1/4 teaspoon cinnamon

Mix all the streusel ingredients with your fingers or a fork until crumbly. Make an indentation in the tops of the unbaked muffins. Place a spoonful of streusel mixture in each. Bake as above.

🌸 Blueberry Muffins

I prefer the large, cultivated blueberries for muffins, but wild ones are also fine.

Preheat the oven to 400°F. Grease a muffin pan for 8 large or 12 medium muffins.

1½ cups flour	1 egg, slightly beaten
½ cup sugar	½ teaspoon vanilla
2½ teaspoons baking powder	½ cup milk
½ teaspoon salt	1 cup blueberries
4 tablespoons butter or margarine, softened	1 to 1½ tablespoons cinnamon sugar

Sift the flour, sugar, baking powder, and salt together into a large mixing bowl. Add the butter, egg, vanilla, and milk and cut in with a pastry blender or two knives only until the ingredients are blended, not smooth. Carefully stir in the blueberries. Spoon into the prepared pan. Sprinkle with the cinnamon sugar and bake at 400°F for about 20 minutes.

NOTE: I keep cinnamon sugar mixed up at our house because we all like it on our toast. If you don't have any on hand, mix 1 tablespoon sugar and ¼ teaspoon cinnamon. This amount is ample for the tops of these muffins.

Bran Muffins with Apples and Raisins

These muffins were an afterthought when I was almost through with the bread chapter. I made a double batch at least six times and never threw a muffin away. The always-hungry farm crew thought they were terrific. I'd appear with the muffins still in the pans and hand them out as I walked through the buildings.

Preheat the oven to 400°F. Grease a muffin pan for 8 large or 12 medium muffins.

1 cup bran cereal (not flakes)	2 teaspoons baking powder
1 cup (scant) milk	1 teaspoon baking soda
1 egg	$\frac{1}{2}$ teaspoon salt
$\frac{1}{3}$ cup lightly packed dark brown sugar	$\frac{1}{4}$ teaspoon cinnamon
4 tablespoons butter or margarine, softened	$\frac{3}{4}$ cup peeled, $\frac{1}{4}$-inch-diced apple
1 cup flour	$\frac{1}{3}$ cup seedless raisins

Pour the milk over the bran cereal and let soak for 5 minutes. Beat the egg, brown sugar, and butter together with an electric mixer until smooth. Using low speed, beat in the bran and milk combination. When blended, sift the flour, baking powder, baking soda, salt, and cinnamon together and stir into the bran mixture. Stir in the apple and raisins. Spoon into the prepared pan and bake at 400°F for approximately 20 minutes.

NOTE: If you are like me, you are more likely to have raisin bran than other bran cereals on your shelf. If you do, and want to use it, use the same recipe, substituting $1\frac{2}{3}$ cups raisin bran for the 1 cup bran cereal and using only $\frac{1}{4}$ cup raisins (there are already some in the cereal). The amount of milk and other ingredients remains the same.

❧Carrot-Oatmeal Muffins

These muffins are made with grated raw, not cooked, carrot, so they can be prepared at the last minute.

Preheat the oven to 400°F. Grease a muffin pan for 8 large or 12 medium muffins.

*1/3 cup butter or margarine,
  softened*
1 egg
*3/4 cup lightly packed dark
  brown sugar*
3/4 cup milk
1 cup finely grated carrot
1 cup quick-cooking oatmeal

1 1/4 cups flour
2 1/2 teaspoons baking powder
1/2 teaspoon salt
*1/2 teaspoon allspice (or
  cinnamon)*
2/3 cup raisins (optional)

Beat the butter, egg, and brown sugar together with an electric mixer until the mixture is smooth. Stir the milk, carrot, and oatmeal into the butter mixture. Sift the flour, baking powder, salt, and allspice together and combine the two mixtures. Stir in the raisins. Bake at 400°F for approximately 20 minutes in the prepared pan.

❧Pumpkin or Winter Squash Muffins

Preheat the oven to 400°F. Grease a muffin pan for 8 large or 12 medium muffins.

1 1/2 cups flour
1/2 cup sugar
1/2 teaspoon salt
2 1/2 teaspoons baking powder
1/2 teaspoon cinnamon
1/4 teaspoon nutmeg
1/8 teaspoon cloves

1 egg, beaten
*4 tablespoons butter or
  margarine, melted and cooled*
1/2 cup milk
*3/4 cup cooked and mashed
  pumpkin or squash*

Sift the flour, sugar, salt, baking powder, cinnamon, nutmeg, and cloves into a large mixing bowl. Thoroughly mix the remaining ingredients in another bowl. Stir the milk mixture into the dry ingredients until the dry ingredients are moistened. Do not beat. Spoon into the prepared pan. Bake at 400°F for approximately 20 minutes.

❧ Cranberry Muffins

Preheat the oven to 400°F. Grease a muffin pan for 8 large or 12 medium muffins.

1 cup coarsely chopped cranberries	⅓ cup butter or margarine, softened
⅔ cup sugar	1 egg
2 cups flour	¾ cup milk
3 teaspoons baking powder	1 teaspoon vanilla
½ teaspoon salt	¼ cup chopped nuts
¼ teaspoon cinnamon	

Mix the cranberries and ⅓ cup of the sugar and set aside. Sift the flour, the remaining ⅓ cup sugar, baking powder, salt, and cinnamon together into a large mixing bowl. Cut the butter into the dry ingredients with a pastry blender or two knives. Beat the egg, milk, and vanilla together in another bowl, then stir them into the flour mixture. Stir the nuts and the reserved chopped cranberries and sugar into the batter. Spoon into the prepared pan. Bake at 400°F for approximately 20 minutes.

❦ *Parsnip Sour Cream Muffins*

This is a "try it, you'll like it" recipe, with parsnips the secret ingredient. You may want to use less sugar if your parsnips are especially sweet. The sour cream makes these muffins tender and delicious.

Preheat the oven to 400°F. Grease a muffin pan for 8 large or 12 medium muffins.

1 egg, beaten
½ cup sour cream
⅔ cup cooked and puréed or well-mashed parsnip
2 tablespoons butter or margarine, melted
⅓ cup milk
1½ cups flour
½ cup sugar
1½ teaspoons baking powder

½ teaspoon baking soda
½ teaspoon salt
½ teaspoon cinnamon
¼ teaspoon nutmeg
¼ teaspoon ginger
⅛ teaspoon cloves
2 tablespoons cinnamon sugar or plain sugar (optional)

Place the egg, sour cream, parsnip, butter, and milk in a bowl and mix thoroughly. Sift the flour, sugar, baking powder, baking soda, salt, cinnamon, nutmeg, ginger, and cloves into a large mixing bowl. Stir the egg mixture into the dry ingredients. This is a very thick batter. Spoon into the prepared pan. Sprinkle the tops of the muffins with cinnamon sugar or plain sugar. Bake at 400°F for 20 to 25 minutes.

❧ Double Corn Muffins

Use both cornmeal and fresh corn kernels to make these muffins. Cut the kernels off young, sweet ears of corn for the best-tasting muffins.

Preheat the oven to 400°F. Grease a muffin pan for 8 large or 12 medium muffins.

1 cup fresh corn kernels	¾ teaspoon salt
¾ cup yellow cornmeal	⅓ cup butter or margarine, softened
1 cup flour	
⅓ cup sugar	⅔ cup milk
4 teaspoons baking powder	1 egg, beaten

Before you start, cut the kernels off 3 or 4 ears of corn to get 1 cup of kernels. Set aside.

Sift the cornmeal, flour, sugar, baking powder, and salt into a large mixing bowl. Cut in the butter with a pastry blender or two knives. Mix the milk and egg and stir them in only until the dry ingredients are moistened, not smooth. Stir in the corn kernels. Spoon the batter into the prepared pan. Bake at 400°F for about 20 minutes.

❧ Apple Bread

This moist bread is made with raw apple. If you're tired of banana or pumpkin bread, try it for a nice change.

Preheat the oven to 350°F. Grease a 9-by-5-inch loaf pan.

½ cup oil	½ teaspoon salt
2 eggs	1 teaspoon cinnamon
¾ cup sugar	½ teaspoon nutmeg
1½ cups flour	2 cups peeled, coarsely chopped raw apple
1¼ teaspoons baking soda	
1 teaspoon baking powder	½ cup chopped walnuts

Using an electric mixer, beat the oil, eggs, and sugar together until thoroughly blended. Sift the flour, baking soda, baking powder, salt, cinnamon, and nutmeg together and stir into the egg mixture. Add the apple and nuts. Place in the prepared pan and bake at 350°F for approximately 50 minutes.

❧ Cranberry-Banana Bread

Preheat the oven to 350°F. Grease a 9-by-5-inch loaf pan.

¼ cup butter or margarine, softened
1 cup sugar
2 eggs
½ cup mashed banana
1 cup coarsely chopped cranberries
¼ cup water

1 teaspoon vanilla
1¾ cups flour
1½ teaspoons baking powder
½ teaspoon baking soda
1 teaspoon salt
½ teaspoon cinnamon
½ cup chopped nuts

Cream the butter and sugar in a large mixing bowl. Beat in the eggs with an electric mixer. Stir in the banana, cranberries, water, and vanilla. Sift the flour, baking powder, baking soda, salt, and cinnamon together and stir them into the batter. Add the chopped nuts. Pour into the prepared pan and bake at 350°F for approximately 55 minutes.

❀ Cranberry-Orange Bread

When I was testing cranberry breads, I took a selection down on a bread board and asked the farm crew to write down their preference. No one could decide between the cranberry-orange and cranberry-banana breads so, not wanting any disagreement, I have included both.

Preheat the oven to 350°F. Grease a 9-by-5-inch loaf pan.

2 cups flour
1 cup sugar
1½ teaspoons baking powder
½ teaspoon baking soda
1 teaspoon salt
¼ cup butter or margarine, softened

½ cup orange juice
1½ teaspoons grated orange peel
2 eggs, beaten
1½ cups coarsely chopped cranberries
½ cup chopped nuts

Sift the flour, sugar, baking powder, baking soda, and salt together into a mixing bowl. Cut in the butter with a pastry blender or two knives. Combine the orange juice, peel, and eggs and stir them into the flour-butter mixture. Add the cranberries and nuts. Place in the prepared pan and bake at 350°F for approximately 55 minutes.

✿ *Pumpkin or Squash Bread*

This dark, moist bread is my favorite. It is delicious plain with a cup of coffee or spread with cream cheese and made into little sandwiches for a party. Make sure you slice it with a very sharp knife because of the raisins. When I have a buffet dinner for guests, I usually make a selection of quick breads for my bread basket. It's easier than trying to serve hot rolls, is always popular, and the bread can be made the day before the party.

Preheat the oven to 350°F. Grease a 9-by-5-inch loaf pan.

⅓ cup butter or margarine, softened
1⅓ cups sugar
2 eggs
1 cup cooked, mashed pumpkin or winter squash
¼ cup water
1⅔ cups flour
¼ teaspoon baking powder

1 teaspoon baking soda
¾ teaspoon salt
¾ teaspoon nutmeg
½ teaspoon cinnamon
½ teaspoon cloves
½ cup chopped walnuts
½ cup seedless raisins

Cream the butter and sugar. Beat in the eggs with an electric mixer. Beat in the pumpkin and water until smooth. Sift the flour, baking powder, baking soda, salt, nutmeg, cinnamon, and cloves together. Beat the dry ingredients into the pumpkin mixture. Stir the walnuts and raisins into the batter. Place in the prepared pan and bake at 350°F for approximately one hour.

✿ Zucchini Bread

This recipe makes two loaves that are smaller than the other breads in this book. Use two 8-by-4-inch or 1½-quart loaf pans.

Preheat the oven to 350°F. Grease two 1½-quart loaf pans.

3 eggs
1⅔ cups sugar
1 cup oil
1½ teaspoons vanilla
3 cups flour
1 teaspoon baking powder
1 teaspoon baking soda
1 teaspoon salt

2 teaspoons cinnamon
1 teaspoon nutmeg
¾ cup chopped nuts
2 cups lightly packed coarsely shredded zucchini
1 cup seedless raisins (optional)

Beat the eggs slightly in a large mixing bowl, then beat in the sugar, oil, and vanilla until very well mixed. Sift the flour, baking powder, baking soda, salt, cinnamon, and nutmeg together and beat into the first mixture until smooth. Stir in the nuts, zucchini, and raisins. This batter is very thick, but the zucchini provides moisture. Place in the prepared pans and bake at 350°F for approximately 1 hour.

🌸 *Blueberry Coffee Cake*

Preheat the oven to 350°F. Grease an 8-inch-square baking dish.

STREUSEL TOPPING

3 tablespoons butter or
   margarine, softened
$\frac{1}{4}$ cup sugar
$\frac{1}{3}$ cup flour

$\frac{1}{4}$ cup chopped walnuts
$\frac{1}{4}$ teaspoon cinnamon

Mix all the ingredients with a fork or your fingers to make streusel crumbs. Set aside.

COFFEE CAKE

$\frac{2}{3}$ cup sugar
$\frac{1}{3}$ cup butter or margarine,
   softened
2 eggs
$\frac{1}{2}$ cup milk
$1\frac{1}{2}$ cups flour

$1\frac{1}{2}$ teaspoons baking powder
1 teaspoon baking soda
$\frac{1}{2}$ teaspoon salt
$\frac{1}{2}$ teaspoon cinnamon
1 cup blueberries

Cream the sugar and butter in a large mixing bowl. Beat in the eggs with an electric mixer and then stir in the milk. Sift the flour, baking powder, baking soda, salt, and cinnamon together and stir them in. Carefully stir in $\frac{1}{2}$ cup of the blueberries. Spread the batter in the prepared pan. Top with the remaining $\frac{1}{2}$ cup berries. Sprinkle the topping mixture over the cake. Bake at 350°F for about 35 to 40 minutes. Serve warm.

❧Cranberry Coffee Cake

Preheat the oven to 350°F. Grease an 8-inch-square cake pan.

3 tablespoons butter or
   margarine, softened
1½ cups sugar
2 eggs
1 teaspoon vanilla
½ cup sour cream
1⅔ cups flour

1½ teaspoons baking powder
1 teaspoon baking soda
¾ teaspoon salt
1 cup coarsely chopped
   cranberries (lightly packed)
½ cup chopped nuts
½ teaspoon cinnamon

Cream the butter with 1 cup of the sugar in a large mixing bowl. Beat in the eggs and vanilla with an electric mixer. Add the sour cream and stir until well blended. Sift the flour, baking powder, baking soda, and salt together and stir into the liquid ingredients. Combine the cranberries, nuts, and ⅓ cup of the sugar in another bowl. Stir the cranberry mixture into the batter. Spread the batter in the prepared pan. Mix the cinnamon with 2 tablespoons of the sugar to make cinnamon sugar and sprinkle it over the batter. Bake at 350°F for 35 to 40 minutes. Serve warm with butter.

❀ *Peach Upside-Down Coffee Cake*

This recipe is a variation of the old-fashioned pineapple upside-down cake that I loved as a child. Now that I'm grown up, I prefer peach upside-down cake with my coffee in the morning. You can serve it warm, topped with whipped cream for dessert, but the cake isn't quite sweet enough for a dessert cake.

Preheat the oven to 350°F. Butter an 8- or 9-inch square baking pan.

3 tablespoons butter or
   margarine, melted
1/3 cup lightly packed light or
   dark brown sugar
2 cups peeled, sliced ripe
   peaches
1/3 cup chopped walnuts or
   pecans
1/4 cup butter or margarine,
   softened
3/4 cup sugar

2 eggs
3/4 cup sour cream
1 teaspoon vanilla
1 1/2 cups flour
1 teaspoon baking powder
1 teaspoon baking soda
1/2 teaspoon salt
1/4 teaspoon nutmeg

Melt the 3 tablespoons of butter in a small saucepan over low heat and stir in the brown sugar. When blended, pour into the prepared pan. Spread the mixture as evenly as possible. Arrange the sliced peaches on top in a single layer and sprinkle the peaches with the chopped nuts. Set aside while you prepare the batter.

Cream the 1/4 cup of butter with the sugar in a large mixing bowl. Beat in the eggs, one at a time, with an electric mixer. Stir in the sour cream and vanilla. Sift the flour, baking powder, baking soda, salt, and nutmeg together and add to the batter, stirring until very well mixed. The batter should be very thick. Carefully spread the batter over the peaches. Bake at 350°F for approximately 35 minutes. Run a knife around the edges and immediately turn the cake upside down on a plate or cookie sheet. It should fall out of the pan with the peaches on top. Remove the pan and let the cake cool slightly before serving.

❧ Streusel-Topped Rhubarb Coffee Cake

It's a shame that the season for fresh rhubarb is so short. But you can easily extend the season by freezing a supply for future use.

Preheat the oven to 350°F. Grease and flour an 8-by-11-inch baking pan.

STREUSEL TOPPING

3 tablespoons butter or
  margarine, softened
⅓ cup flour
½ cup lightly packed brown
  sugar

½ cup chopped nuts
1 teaspoon cinnamon

Mix all the ingredients with a fork or your fingers until crumbly. Set aside.

COFFEE CAKE

½ cup butter or margarine,
  softened
1 cup sugar
1 egg
½ cup milk
1 teaspoon vanilla
1½ cups flour

2½ teaspoons baking powder
½ teaspoon salt
1 teaspoon cinnamon
¼ teaspoon nutmeg
2 cups ¼-inch pieces rhubarb

Cream the butter with the sugar in a large mixing bowl. Beat in the egg with an electric mixer. Add the milk and vanilla and stir until well blended. Sift the flour, baking powder, salt, cinnamon, and nutmeg together and stir them into the batter. Stir in the rhubarb. Spread the batter in the prepared pan. Top with the streusel. Bake at 350°F for approximately 40 minutes. Let cool for about 20 minutes before serving.

❧ Apple Pancakes

Apple Pancakes are great for breakfast on Sunday mornings or any time a special treat is in order. Several students from a fifth-grade class came to my house to do some cooking, and this was a favorite recipe. As a matter of fact, we mixed several batches of batter, took electric frying pans to school, and cooked pancakes for the whole class. The pancakes were a huge success.

1 egg	3 tablespoons sugar
1 cup milk	1/4 teaspoon cinnamon
3 tablespoons butter or	Dash nutmeg
margarine, melted	1 1/4 cups peeled, chopped apple
1 1/2 cups flour	(1 large)
2 1/2 teaspoons baking powder	
1/2 teaspoon salt	

Beat the egg, milk, and melted butter together with an eggbeater until well blended. Sift the flour, baking powder, salt, sugar, cinnamon, and nutmeg together. Stir the dry ingredients into the liquid until moistened. Stir in the chopped apple. Heat a large frying pan over medium-high, grease it lightly, and cook the pancakes, turning once after bubbles form on top of the pancakes. Serve with butter and syrup or honey.

NOTE: The pancakes will be better if you don't blend the liquid and flour mixtures until you are ready to cook them.

🌸 Blueberry Pancakes

My most faithful tasters at the farm, Nancy MacLauchlan and Cindy Wilson, couldn't agree as to whether pancakes should be thick or thin. Not wanting to create further dissension, I took the middle-of-the-road route with this recipe. If you prefer thick pancakes, use less milk; for thin ones, use more.

1⅓ cups milk
  1 tablespoon lemon juice
1½ cups flour
  ¼ cup sugar
1½ teaspoons baking powder
 ½ teaspoon baking soda
 ½ teaspoon salt

⅛ teaspoon cinnamon
 3 tablespoons oil or melted butter
 1 egg
¾ cup wild blueberries (1 cup large berries)

Combine the milk and lemon juice and set aside for 10 minutes to make sour milk. Sift the flour, sugar, baking powder, baking soda, salt, and cinnamon into a large mixing bowl. Beat the sour milk, oil, and egg together with a wire whisk or fork. Stir into the dry ingredients only until moist. Don't try to eliminate all the lumps. Stir in the blueberries. Heat a large frying pan and brush it with oil. Cook the pancakes on one side until bubbles form, turn, and continue to cook the second side until the pancakes are done. Serve with butter and syrup.

❀ Fresh Corn Pancakes or Fritters

You can deep-fry these pancakes to make fritters, but I find it easier to cook them in a frying pan. Put enough batter in the pan to form 2-inch-diameter patties. Serve them with syrup as you would fritters, perhaps in place of bread with a simple meal. If you want to serve Corn Pancakes for breakfast, increase the amount of milk a bit to thin the batter.

1½ cups corn kernels (about 6 ears, depending on size)	1 tablespoon sugar
1 egg	1½ teaspoons baking powder
⅓ cup milk	¾ teaspoon salt
1 cup flour	1 tablespoon butter, melted

Cut enough corn off the cobs to make 1½ cups corn kernels.

Beat the egg in a mixing bowl and stir in the corn kernels and milk. Sift the flour, sugar, baking powder, and salt together and stir them into the milk mixture. Add the melted butter. Mix well, as the batter should be very thick. Deep-fry or cook in 2-inch-diameter patties in a large frying pan containing about ⅛ inch of fat. Serve as a side dish with maple syrup.

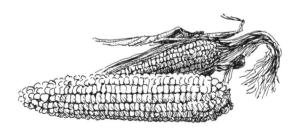

❧ Winter Squash Pancakes

MAKES ABOUT 12 2½- TO 3-INCH PANCAKES

These pancakes are considerably more interesting than plain ones
and are good for Halloween or Thanksgiving breakfast. Serve them
just with butter or with butter and syrup. Any cooked, mashed
winter squash — for example, butternut, hubbard — or pumpkin
can be used.

2 eggs	¼ cup sugar
⅔ cup cooked, mashed winter squash or pumpkin	¾ teaspoon salt
	2½ teaspoons baking powder
3 tablespoons oil	1¼ teaspoons cinnamon
1 cup milk	1 teaspoon nutmeg
1½ cups flour	

Beat the eggs in a large mixing bowl. Stir in the squash, oil, and
milk. Sift the flour, sugar, salt, baking powder, cinnamon, and nutmeg together and stir into the milk mixture. Heat a frying pan
over medium-high, grease it lightly, and cook the pancakes, turning
once after bubbles form on top.

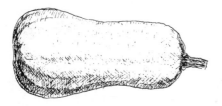

❧ Squash or Pumpkin Pecan Waffles

MAKES 4 LARGE WAFFLES

For a new twist to your breakfast menu, try these waffles. They have to cook at medium heat a little longer than conventional waffles if you want them to be crisp. As you finish each, keep them warm on a rack in a 200°F oven until time to serve. It's important to keep them on a rack so that the bottoms don't become soggy.

Preheat the waffle iron.

1½ cups flour
¼ cup sugar
3 teaspoons baking powder
¾ teaspoon salt
1¼ teaspoons cinnamon
¾ teaspoon nutmeg
2 eggs, separated

1¼ cups milk
½ cup vegetable oil or melted butter
¾ cup cooked, puréed winter squash or pumpkin
⅓ cup finely chopped pecans

Sift the flour, sugar, baking powder, salt, cinnamon, and nutmeg into a large mixing bowl. Thoroughly mix the egg yolks, milk, oil, and squash in another bowl. Stir the liquid mixture into the dry ingredients. Do not beat. Add the pecans. Beat the egg whites until stiff and fold them in just before cooking. Cook waffles in the prepared waffle iron according to the manufacturer's instructions.

4

*Salads
and
Relishes*

There are so many different types of salads from which to choose that I had a problem deciding which to include. I also serve side dishes like rhubarb sauce, applesauce, and spiced fruit in place of salad, especially if I'm planning to have cooked greens with dinner. Therefore, you will find in this chapter not only recipes for green salads and jellied fruit salads, but also recipes for other accompaniments to meals.

Many vegetables that are normally cooked are surprisingly versatile. For example, raw parsnip and winter squash make good grated salads. They are excellent in tossed salad, as are raw zucchini or summer squash, kohlrabi, cauliflower, broccoli, and yellow or white turnip. Tossed salads are always better when you include a mixture of greens. Use your imagination and add to your salads a small amount of arugula (a sharp-tasting leafy vegetable sometimes used by itself for salad), small beet greens, watercress, or Belgian endive.

The old standby, iceberg lettuce, which is a staple in this country, is not as popular elsewhere. A friend of ours from the Netherlands thinks that iceberg lettuce is absolutely unbeatable. Iceberg is not generally available in his country, so that's what he wants in his salad when he's here. On the other hand, it is hard for him to understand why I like salads made with Boston lettuce, because Dutch greenhouses produce a great deal of Boston lettuce, which is a staple in salads there. Which only shows that what you put in your salads is all a matter of personal taste (and availability). The following are major types of lettuce grown and available in the Northeast:

Iceberg or Crisphead
Iceberg is still the most popular type of lettuce, but, in the Boston area, loose-leaf lettuces are catching up in popularity. Our locally

grown iceberg tends to be a looser head than that grown in other parts of the country. It is a firm, crisp lettuce that I generally combine with other varieties in tossed salads.

Romaine

Like iceberg, romaine has more body than the softer Boston or leaf lettuces, so it stands up to heavy dressings. It is almost always used to make Caesar Salad. It is my favorite, and I often toss it with sliced fresh mushrooms and shredded Swiss cheese. Lightly dressed with vinaigrette or Italian dressing, it's a simple but delightful salad.

Boston or Butterhead

Since this head lettuce is fragile, I don't use my salad spinner to dry it. I wash each leaf and layer the leaves with paper towels before refrigerating. The delicate flavor is so good that I sometimes eat it leaf by leaf as a snack. Use a light dressing on this lettuce so the dressing won't overpower its flavor.

Loose-Leaf Lettuce

Salad Bowl, Green Ice, Grand Rapids, and Ruby are some of the many varieties of this popular leaf-type lettuce. While any of these varieties is lovely served alone, I usually mix them with other greens (especially the red for color) to enhance my salads. As with Boston lettuce, you must take care not to overpower the flavor with a heavy dressing.

All these lettuces, including loose-leaf, are now available year round. During the colder months, they are grown in California and Arizona and shipped to our area, and to all parts of the United States.

🌿 Boston Lettuce with Hot Bacon Dressing

SERVES ABOUT 4

Make this salad and the one following with a loose-head, soft lettuce like Boston or Bibb. It isn't a good salad for a crowd, because it has to be prepared at the last minute. Plan to serve it as a first course so it can be eaten while the dressing is still warm.

4 slices bacon, crisply cooked
  and crumbled
2 tablespoons bacon fat
2 tablespoons minced onion
2 tablespoons cider vinegar

1 tablespoon packed dark
  brown sugar
1/2 teaspoon dry mustard
1/4 teaspoon salt
1 medium head Boston lettuce

Cook the bacon. Remove it from the heat and crumble, leaving 2 tablespoons of bacon fat in the frying pan.

Wash, dry, and tear the lettuce into small pieces, and place it in a large bowl. Sprinkle the bacon pieces over the lettuce.

Heat the reserved bacon fat. Add the onion and cook for 30 seconds; add the vinegar, sugar, mustard, and salt, and bring the mixture to a boil. Pour the hot dressing over the lettuce and bacon pieces and mix thoroughly. Serve immediately.

Wilted Sweet-and-Sour Boston Lettuce

SERVES 4 TO 6

It's hard to say which wilted salad I like better, but I think this one might just have the edge over the previous one. Both are better before a meal, or after the main course in the European fashion, rather than with the main course, because they should be eaten immediately after they are prepared. Be forewarned: The cooked dressing for this salad looks somewhat curdled, but it tastes excellent.

4 slices bacon, crisply cooked
   and crumbled
   Bacon fat
1 egg
2 tablespoons cider vinegar
1 tablespoon sugar

¼ teaspoon salt
⅛ teaspoon pepper
¼ cup light cream
1 large head Boston lettuce

Cook the bacon, remove it from the frying pan and crumble, reserving all the bacon fat in the pan.

Beat the egg, vinegar, sugar, salt, pepper, and cream together and set aside.

Wash, dry, and tear the lettuce into small pieces and put it into a large bowl.

Return the bacon fat to the heat. When it is hot, pour it over the lettuce. Mix well. Pour the egg mixture into the same pan and cook over medium heat until it boils and thickens, stirring constantly. Pour the hot sweet-and-sour mixture over the lettuce and stir well. Serve immediately.

🌿 Caesar Salad

SERVES 6 TO 8

Waiters in elegant restaurants sometimes make a production of creating this famous salad at your table. I've simplified the recipe to make it easier to serve at home. I like raw egg in the salad, but I beat it well. You won't find anchovies in my recipe, but if you like, chop them and add with the cheese and croutons.

1 head romaine lettuce
1 small clove garlic
1/2 teaspoon salt
1/4 teaspoon pepper
1/4 cup lemon juice
1 teaspoon Worcestershire sauce
1 egg

3/4 cup oil, olive or salad or combination
1/3 cup grated Parmesan or Romano cheese
2 cups croutons (recipe, page 117)

Wash and dry the romaine and remove the heavy center ribs from the larger leaves, if desired. Tear the leaves into small, but larger than bite-sized, pieces. Place the lettuce in the refrigerator to chill.

Chop the clove of garlic and place it in a small mixing bowl. Add the salt and pepper, and, using a fork, mash them with the garlic. Add the lemon juice, Worcestershire, and egg, and, using a fork or wire whisk, whip them until thoroughly blended. Slowly pour in the oil, beating constantly.

Sprinkle the cheese over the lettuce, toss with the dressing, and add the croutons. Serve immediately.

NOTE: Don't add all the dressing at once because, depending on the size of the head of lettuce, you may not need all of it. Leftover dressing should be refrigerated.

❧ Spinach Salad

MAKES ABOUT 8 SIDE-DISH OR 3 TO 4 MAIN-COURSE
LUNCHEON SALADS

Spinach Salad is best when the leaves are small. However, it is good whenever the spinach is fresh and crisp. If the leaves are too large, tear them into smaller pieces so the salad is easier to manage. This is a favorite salad around the farm and I make it often for parties. Add the bacon, croutons, and dressing just before serving, so the croutons don't become soggy.

1½ pounds untrimmed spinach
    (1 pound trimmed)
  3 finely chopped hard-boiled
    eggs
 10 slices bacon, crisply cooked
    and crumbled
 ¼ cup grated Parmesan or
    Romano cheese

1½ cups garlic croutons (recipe,
    page 117)
  2 cups sliced mushrooms
    Italian or Vinaigrette
    Dressing (recipe, page 116)
    to coat

Trim the roots and stems from the spinach well ahead of serving time. Wash it thoroughly, drain well, and chill.

Hard-boil the eggs, chill, and chop. Cook the bacon and make the croutons. Don't slice the mushrooms until close to serving time.

When you're ready to serve, mix all the ingredients and toss with enough of the vinaigrette (or bottled Italian salad dressing) to coat the spinach thoroughly.

🌿 Marinated Mushroom Salad

We may not grow mushrooms, but we sure sell them in large quantities. This salad, which also uses green and red peppers, should be made early in the day or the day before you plan to serve it. It looks lovely on individual salad plates atop loose-leaf lettuce and is an interesting addition to a buffet table. If you like, stir in a cup of cheese cubes, either Swiss or cheddar.

1 pound mushrooms, trimmed and cut into 1/4-inch slices	1 teaspoon finely minced garlic
1/2 cup red wine vinegar	1/2 red onion, thinly sliced (about 1/4 pound)
3/4 cup salad oil	2 sweet peppers in thin strips (1 red and 1 green)
1 teaspoon salt	
1/2 teaspoon ground pepper	

Place the sliced mushrooms in a glass or stainless-steel mixing bowl. Mix the vinegar, oil, salt, pepper, and garlic in a small saucepan. Bring to a boil over high heat and pour it over the sliced mushrooms. Stir until the mushrooms are well coated with the hot dressing. Add the sliced onion and peppers. Stir, cover, and refrigerate, stirring occasionally, for at least 6 hours or overnight. Drain before serving.

🌿 Marinated Zucchini and Summer Squash

SERVES 6 TO 8

Here is a different and easy salad or side dish for your summer barbecue. It can be made with one or the other squash, but it is much more attractive if you use a combination.

1½ pounds squash, thinly sliced
(1 zucchini and 1 summer,
each about ¾ pounds)
4 small white boiling onions,
peeled and thinly sliced into
rings
½ cup salad oil

⅓ cup white wine vinegar
1 teaspoon minced garlic
¾ teaspoon salt
⅛ teaspoon ground pepper
¼ teaspoon celery seed
¼ teaspoon sugar

Place the squash and onions in a 3-quart stainless-steel saucepan.
Mix the remaining ingredients in a bowl, and pour them over the
squash. Stir to coat the squash. Cover and bring the mixture to a
boil over medium heat. Remove the cover and cook, stirring, only
until the squash is heated through, not cooked.

Remove from the heat and place in a stainless-steel or glass bowl
(hot marinade and all). Cover and marinate overnight or for at
least 6 hours in the refrigerator. Stir occasionally. Serve chilled.

✽ Marinated Tomato Slices with Fresh Basil

SERVES 4 TO 6

We prefer our tomatoes (and most fruits) at room temperature,
since chilling seems to diminish the flavor. Therefore, I usually
serve these at room temperature on a bed of loose-leaf lettuce.

2 large, ripe tomatoes (1 to 1½
pounds total)
2 tablespoons chopped fresh
basil
3 tablespoons salad or olive oil

2 tablespoons lemon juice
½ teaspoon salt
⅛ teaspoon freshly ground
pepper
½ teaspoon sugar

Slice the tomatoes into a deep dish or glass pie plate. Sprinkle the
slices with the chopped basil. Mix the remaining ingredients with
a wire whisk or fork. Pour this dressing over the tomatoes. Marinate for at least 1 hour at room temperature, spooning the dressing over the tomatoes occasionally. Serve at room temperature or
chilled.

🐚 Cucumber and Sour Cream Salad

SERVES 6 TO 8

This salad is good in the summer, when cucumbers are especially flavorful. You have to salt the cucumbers so they can absorb the sour cream flavor and lose their crispness.

    4 large cucumbers (about 2
        pounds)
 1½ tablespoons salt

Peel the cucumbers and slice them into rounds. Place them in a colander and sprinkle with the salt. Let the cucumbers sit and drain for 1 hour. Thoroughly rinse off the salt and pat the slices dry with paper towels. Make one of the following dressings and pour it over the cucumbers. Stir to coat and refrigerate for at least 2 hours before serving.

Sour Cream and Horseradish

    1 cup sour cream
 ¼ teaspoon salt (if necessary)
    Freshly ground pepper to taste

    1 tablespoon finely minced
        onion
 1 to 2 tablespoons grated
        horseradish, fresh or
        bottled (more, if desired)

Mix all the ingredients thoroughly.

Sour Cream and Dill

    1 cup sour cream
    2 teaspoons vinegar
 ½ teaspoon sugar
    1 tablespoon finely minced
        onion

    2 tablespoons chopped fresh
        dill
 ⅛ teaspoon freshly ground
        pepper

Mix all the ingredients thoroughly.

🌱 Minted Pea and Radish Salad

SERVES 4 TO 6

Peas and radishes offer an attractive color contrast for an interesting spring salad. Be careful not to overdo the mint as it should be a hint of, rather than an overpowering, flavor.

1 cup water
1 teaspoon salt
2 cups shelled peas
1 cup thinly sliced radishes
3 tablespoons thinly sliced scallions

½ cup chopped celery
1 teaspoon finely chopped fresh mint
1 tablespoon mayonnaise
2 tablespoons sour cream
Dash freshly ground pepper

Place the water and salt in a 2-quart saucepan and bring to a boil. Add the peas and cook them until they are barely tender (about 4 minutes for fresh peas). Immediately run cold water over the peas to stop the cooking. Drain the peas very well.

Mix the peas, radishes, scallions, celery, and mint. Chill for at least 1 hour. Just before serving, stir in the mayonnaise, sour cream, and pepper. Serve on a bed of lettuce surrounded by wedges of tomato or hard-boiled eggs, if desired.

NOTE: Don't add salt to the finished salad because salted radishes give off liquid and make the dressing runny. That is the reason you use a full teaspoon of salt in cooking the peas. One tablespoon of chopped fresh dill may be substituted for the mint.

🐄 Carrot-Raisin-Nut Salad

SERVES 6

Somehow, this salad is one of those old favorites that I forget about. That's a mistake, because it really is very popular, especially with young people.

4 cups peeled, shredded carrots
(about 1 pound without
tops)
½ cup chopped walnuts
½ cup seedless raisins
2 teaspoons sugar

¼ teaspoon salt
¼ teaspoon cinnamon
Dash nutmeg
3 tablespoons orange juice
⅓ cup mayonnaise

Mix the carrots, walnuts, raisins, sugar, salt, cinnamon, nutmeg, and orange juice very well. Stir in the mayonnaise. Chill for at least 1 hour before serving.

🐄 Grated Winter Squash Salad

SERVES 4 TO 6

Squash Salad is similar to carrot, but it's a nice change. Any squash will work, but butternut is particularly good. If you make this salad in the fall when the squash has just been harvested, the squash will be sweet and your salad tasty.

1 pound peeled squash, grated
(4 to 5 cups)
⅓ cup mayonnaise
2 tablespoons sour cream
¾ cup seedless raisins

¾ teaspoon salt
⅛ teaspoon freshly ground
pepper
1 tablespoon honey

Mix all the ingredients until very well blended. Chill the salad for at least 1 hour before serving.

❧ Coleslaw

SERVES 8

5 cups thinly sliced (or
   shredded) green cabbage
1 cup thinly sliced (or
   shredded) red cabbage
1 cup peeled and coarsely
   grated carrot
1/2 cup coarsely chopped onion
2 tablespoons cider vinegar

2 teaspoons sugar
1/2 teaspoon salt
1/4 teaspoon pepper
1/8 teaspoon celery seed
   (optional)
1/3 cup sour cream
1/3 cup mayonnaise

Mix the two kinds of cabbage, carrot, and onion in a large bowl.
Place the vinegar, sugar, salt, pepper, celery seed, sour cream, and
mayonnaise in a smaller bowl. Blend them with a wire whisk or
fork. Stir this dressing into the cabbage mixture until well mixed.
Refrigerate for at least 1 hour before serving, stirring occasionally.

NOTE: You can use 1/2 to 2/3 cup mayonnaise and eliminate the
sour cream, if desired.

❧ Potato Salad with Egg

SERVES 6

I like the taste and color of potato salad that includes egg. When I took potato salad samples to the farm, I found that many people agreed with me. You can vary the salad many ways. I sometimes stir in a tablespoon or two of sweet pickle relish for part of the vinegar. Just use your imagination and stir in herbs to your taste, about ½ cup celery or chopped green pepper, or whatever else appeals to you.

*2 pounds white, all-purpose
  potatoes*
3 hard-boiled eggs, chopped
2 tablespoons chopped parsley
¼ cup salad oil

2 tablespoons cider vinegar
1 teaspoon salt
*¼ teaspoon freshly ground
  pepper*
½ cup mayonnaise

Cook the whole, unpeeled potatoes in boiling water until fork-tender. Don't overcook. Drain and cool slightly until cool enough to handle. Peel and cube the potatoes while they are still hot and place them in a large mixing bowl. Add the chopped eggs, parsley, oil, vinegar, salt, and pepper. Stir until well mixed. Let the potatoes marinate for at least 1 hour or until cool. Stir in the mayonnaise and chill before serving.

🌿 Red-Skinned Potato Salad

SERVES 6

My sister-in-law, Barbara Wilson Fuery, prepares delicious potato salad with small red-skinned potatoes. She cooks them whole and slices them unpeeled while still hot. The red skins make a pretty salad and, of course, the potatoes themselves are lovely. You can use Chicken Broth (recipe, page 40) in place of part of the oil or add some broth if the potatoes seem to be dry.

2 pounds red-skinned potatoes
  (not over 2-inch diameter)
3 tablespoons salad oil
1½ tablespoons red wine
  vinegar
1 tablespoon finely minced
  onion
⅓ cup chopped scallions
¾ teaspoon salt
¼ teaspoon freshly ground
  pepper
1 tablespoon chopped parsley
¾ cup mayonnaise (or enough
  to moisten)

Boil the unpeeled potatoes until fork-tender (20 to 25 minutes). Drain, and while they are still hot, slice them into a mixing bowl. Sprinkle the oil and vinegar over the potatoes. Add the onion, scallions, salt, pepper, and parsley. Stir to mix thoroughly. Cover and let marinate for at least 1 hour. Stir in the mayonnaise and correct the seasoning. Chill before serving.

NOTE: Add a small amount of chopped fresh basil, dill, or tarragon to make the salad even tastier.

❧ Colorful Macaroni Salad

This dish serves 10 to 12, so it is good for a party. A spiral maca-roni, like rotini, looks pretty, but elbow works just as well. If you prefer, substitute diced ham for the pepperoni.

1/2 pound macaroni
2 tablespoons salad oil
2 teaspoons wine vinegar
1/3 cup thinly sliced scallions
1/8 teaspoon freshly ground pepper
1 cup peas, blanched in boiling water briefly, 1 to 2 minutes

1 cup 1/4-inch diced red pepper (green will do but red is more colorful)
1 cup diced Swiss or medium sharp cheddar cheese
1 cup diced pepperoni
1/3 cup mayonnaise
Salt and pepper

Cook the macaroni as directed on the package. Drain it well and then add the oil, vinegar, scallions, and pepper to the hot maca-roni. Stir until well mixed. Refrigerate until almost cool, stirring occasionally. Add the remaining ingredients and stir until well mixed. Season to taste. Chill before serving.

NOTE: The red pepper, cheese, and pepperoni should be cut to about the same size.

🦋Rice Salad

Rice Salad serves about 12, so when you're asked to bring something to a cookout or buffet, this is good party fare. Of course, it can also be halved to serve a smaller group. I prefer it with two types of rice, but it can be made with only white.

1 cup uncooked brown rice
1 cup uncooked white rice
4 tablespoons salad oil
1½ tablespoons red wine
   vinegar
¼ cup finely chopped onions
1 cup green pepper ¼-inch-
   diced
1½ cups peeled, seeded, and
   diced tomatoes

3 tablespoons chopped fresh
   basil leaves
½ teaspoon salt (or to taste)
¼ teaspoon ground pepper
¾ cup pine nuts (pignolias)
   that have been lightly toasted
   in the oven

Cook the brown rice and the white rice in separate pans to get approximately 4 cups of cooked rice. Combine the two kinds of rice. While the rice is still hot, stir in all the remaining ingredients, except the pine nuts. Mix thoroughly. Chill the salad, stirring occasionally. Stir in the pine nuts just before serving.

🌱 Parsnip-Apple Salad

SERVES ABOUT 6

Raw parsnips are very good in salad. You can use them like carrots with raisins or like cabbage in coleslaw. Their natural sweetness combines well with fruit. This salad tastes very much like Waldorf Salad (recipe follows). Your family and guests will like it, but they won't be able to guess the secret ingredient.

3 cups peeled shredded parsnip (about 1 pound)	1/3 cup chopped walnuts
1/2 cup chopped celery	2 tablespoons oil and vinegar dressing (bottled Italian is OK)
2 to 3 cups coarsely chopped apples with skin (2 medium)	2/3 cup mayonnaise
	Salt and pepper to taste

Mix the parsnip, celery, apple, walnuts, and oil and vinegar dressing. Stir in only enough mayonnaise to moisten the salad and salt and pepper if necessary. Chill for at least 1 hour before serving.

NOTE: This is a very simple salad, so be sure to use apples with bright red skin for color.

🌱 Waldorf Salad

SERVES ABOUT 6

What a good fall salad! The orange juice not only keeps the apples from discoloring but also adds flavor. Garnish the salad with thin slices of unpeeled red apple for color. Coat the slices with orange juice to keep them white.

4 cups peeled diced apples (3 to 4 — Cortlands are good)	2/3 cup chopped walnuts
3/4 cup orange juice	Dash salt
1 cup diced celery	1/2 cup mayonnaise

Cut up the apples and place them in a mixing bowl with the orange juice. Stir until the apples are coated with juice. Let stand for

5 to 10 minutes, stirring occasionally. Drain the apples very well. Add the remaining ingredients to the apples, using only enough mayonnaise to moisten the salad. Mix well. Chill the salad for at least 1 hour before serving.

🦃 Molded Cranberry Salad

SERVES 12

3 packages unflavored gelatin
1/3 cup cold water
3 cups orange juice
1/2 cup sugar
8 ounces cream cheese, softened

1 cup chopped celery
1 cup chopped walnuts or pecans
2 cups whole cranberry sauce

Sprinkle the gelatin into the water and let stand for 2 or 3 minutes to soften.

Heat the orange juice until almost boiling, remove from the heat, and stir in the sugar and softened gelatin. Stir until the sugar and gelatin are dissolved.

Using an electric mixer on slow speed, beat the cream cheese until smooth. Continue to beat and slowly pour the hot liquid into the cream cheese. When smooth, place the mixture in the refrigerator and chill until it is slightly thick, stirring occasionally. Remove from the refrigerator and stir in the celery, nuts, and cranberry sauce. Pour into a 2-quart mold or a 9-by-13-inch oblong dish. Chill until firm (several hours). Unmold (or cut into squares) and serve.

NOTE: If the salad isn't pink enough to suit you, add a few drops of red food coloring.

🌿 Peach Cream Cheese Salad

Much to the delight of everyone at the farm, it took me several tries to get the amounts of gelatin and peaches exactly right for this salad. Bob Brown, who has been the grower in our green-houses for many years, claimed, after sampling several trial salads, that it was so delicious, it should be served as dessert, not salad. Gelatin salads are a pleasant change from greens during the summer, especially when made with fresh, ripe peaches.

This recipe calls for both puréed and diced peaches, so make sure you have enough ripe peaches on hand. It can be made in a mold and is firm enough to remove easily. However, if salad molds are your downfall, make it in a dish, cut it into squares, and place individual servings on lettuce leaves.

2 envelopes unflavored gelatin	1 cup sugar
1/2 cup cold water	8 ounces cream cheese, softened
2 cups puréed or mashed peaches	2 1/2 cups diced peaches

Mix the gelatin and cold water together and set aside to let the gelatin soften.

Peel and purée enough ripe peaches to make 2 cups.

Place the puréed peaches in a small saucepan and heat them to a simmer. Remove the peaches from the heat and stir in the sugar and softened gelatin, stirring until both have dissolved.

Place the soft cream cheese in a mixing bowl. Using an electric mixer on low speed, blend the hot peach mixture into the cream cheese a little at a time. When they are thoroughly blended, chill until the mixture is slightly thick. Stir in the diced peaches and turn into a 1 1/2-quart mold or a 9-inch-square dish. Refrigerate for at least 4 hours until firm.

🍓Rhubarb-Strawberry Salad

SERVES 6

2 cups ½-inch pieces rhubarb
    (¾ pound untrimmed)
⅓ cup water
1 3-ounce package strawberry-
    flavored gelatin
½ cup sugar

3 ounces cream cheese,
    softened
½ cup cold water
1½ cups sliced fresh strawberries

Place the rhubarb and ⅓ cup water in a small saucepan. Bring to a simmer over medium-low heat. Simmer until the rhubarb is very soft. Remove it from the heat and add the gelatin and sugar, stirring until both are dissolved. Gradually stir the hot mixture into the cream cheese until well blended. Stir in the ½ cup cold water. Chill until partially set.

Stir in the sliced strawberries. Pour the salad into an 8-inch-square pan and chill until set (3 hours or more). Cut into squares and place on lettuce for individual servings.

NOTE: You can also serve this salad as a dessert. Fill six dessert dishes or stemmed glasses after stirring in the strawberries. Chill and top with whipped cream.

🥬 Applesauce

MAKES ABOUT 4 CUPS OF CHUNKY APPLESAUCE

Homemade applesauce tastes so much better than canned and is so simple to prepare that I'm always amazed at how few people cook their own. Because it freezes perfectly, you can always make extra and keep some for the future. I prefer Cortland apples for cooking, but if they aren't available, any type of apple will do. You have to vary the amount of sugar with different apples. You may need more sugar if you use tart apples. Your applesauce will be only as good as the apples you use to make it, so don't use old, bruised ones.

6 large apples (about 2½ pounds total)
½ cup water
½ cup sugar

¼ teaspoon (scant) cinnamon
⅛ teaspoon nutmeg

Peel, core, and slice the apples. Place them in a 3-quart saucepan with the water. Cover and bring to a boil. Lower the heat and cook, covered, until the apples are tender (5 to 10 minutes), stirring once or twice while cooking. Uncover and stir in the sugar, cinnamon, and nutmeg. Continue to cook, uncovered, stirring occasionally, until the sugar and spices are well blended and the applesauce is cooked (2 to 3 minutes). Serve warm or chilled.

Rosy Stewed Apples

These apples are so easy to do and so good that I make them often. They are also a great last-minute addition to a meal, since you can serve them warm. I never seem to plan ahead, so these frequently solve my problem of what to serve when dinner seems less than ample.

½ cup sugar
1 cup water
½ teaspoon cinnamon (more if you prefer)
10 drops red coloring (or whatever it takes to make apples pink)

3 to 4 apples (about 1½ pounds)

Place the sugar, water, cinnamon, and food coloring in a 2-quart saucepan. Bring the mixture to a boil over high heat. Lower the heat and simmer, uncovered, for about 5 minutes.

While the syrup is cooking, peel, core, and cut the apples into quarters or sixths. After the syrup has cooked five minutes, add the apple pieces. Raise the heat so the syrup returns to a boil, and continue to cook, uncovered, until the apples are almost tender (5 to 8 minutes). Stir several times during cooking. Remove from the heat. The apples will continue to cook in the hot syrup. Serve warm or cold, in place of applesauce as a side dish, or with cream or ice cream as dessert.

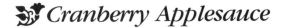 Spiced Peaches and Prune Plums

SERVES 6

Use this spiced fruit in place of applesauce as an accompaniment for meat or poultry. It is somewhat tart, depending on the fruit. Use ripe but not very soft fruit, so it holds its shape when cooked. It can be served chilled or slightly warm, not hot.

1½ pounds unpeeled prune
    plums, halved and seeded
1½ pounds peeled peaches,
    seeded, cut into eighths
¾ to 1 cup sugar

6 whole cloves
½ stick cinnamon
¼ cup water

Place all the ingredients in a 3-quart saucepan. The peaches should be cut into pieces about the size of the plum halves. Cover the pan and bring the mixture to a simmer over medium (not high) heat. Uncover and simmer until the plums and peaches are soft (about 10 minutes). Discard the cloves and cinnamon. The fruit will continue to cook in the hot syrup after the pan is removed from the heat. The plum skins give the fruit a lovely color and are good to eat.

NOTE: You can tie the cloves and cinnamon in cheesecloth so you don't have to search through the fruit for them before serving.

Cranberry Applesauce

MAKES ABOUT 4 CUPS

4 large apples (1½ to 2
    pounds)
1½ to 2 cups whole cranberries
¾ cup water

1 cup sugar
½ teaspoon cinnamon
⅛ teaspoon cloves

Peel, core, and slice the apples and put them into a heavy 2- or 3-quart saucepan with the cranberries and the water. Place them over medium heat and cook, covered, until the apples and cranberries are soft (5 to 10 minutes, depending on the type of apple).

Add the sugar, cinnamon, and cloves and simmer, uncovered, stirring often, until the sugar is well dissolved and the flavors are blended (4 to 5 minutes). Serve chilled.

🥀 Cranberry Orange Sauce

MAKES ABOUT 3½ CUPS

This sauce contains orange juice and a touch of orange liqueur to give a slightly different taste to ordinary cranberry sauce.

¼ cup water
¾ cup orange juice
2 cups sugar (less for tart sauce)
4 cups whole cranberries

1½ teaspoons grated orange rind
1 tablespoon orange-flavored liqueur (optional)

Place the water, orange juice, sugar, cranberries, and orange rind in a 2-quart saucepan. Cover and bring to a boil. Uncover, lower the heat, and simmer until the cranberries burst and the sauce thickens a bit (about 10 minutes). Mash any cranberries that remain whole and remove from the heat. Stir in the orange liqueur. The sauce thickens more as it cools. Chill before serving.

🌱 Rhubarb Sauce

MAKES 2½ TO 3 CUPS

This sauce reminds me of home, since my father grew rhubarb and my mother often served rhubarb sauce with dinner. You may use strawberries in place of some of the rhubarb, but remember to cut down slightly on the sugar.

4 cups cut-up rhubarb (about
   1½ pounds)
3 tablespoons water

1 cup sugar
⅛ teaspoon cinnamon

Cut the rhubarb into ½- to 1-inch lengths and place in a heavy 2-quart saucepan. Add the water, cover, and place over low heat. Cook until the rhubarb softens (about 5 minutes). The heat must be low or the rhubarb will burn. Stir occasionally. Add the sugar and cinnamon. Stir until the sugar dissolves. Simmer, uncovered, for about 5 minutes longer or until the rhubarb is completely cooked. Serve chilled as a side dish or slightly warm on ice cream for dessert.

NOTE: If your rhubarb is not red enough, you may want to add a drop or two or red food coloring.

🌾 Refrigerator Bread-and-Butter Pickles

These are fun to make and good to eat. After three days in the refrigerator, they are ready. They aren't pickles to put away for the winter, but to serve right away.

5 to 6 *pickling cucumbers* *(about 2 pounds)*	2 *teaspoons mustard seed*
4 *small white onions*	¼ *teaspoon ground turmeric*
3 *tablespoons kosher salt*	¼ *teaspoon celery seed*
1 *cup white vinegar*	3 *whole cloves*
¾ *cup sugar*	¼ *cup water*

Wash the cucumbers and slice them thinly into a glass or stainless-steel bowl. Peel the onions and slice them very thinly. Separate the onion slices into rings and add them to the cucumbers. Sprinkle the onions and cucumbers with the salt and mix. Cover with water and let soak for 2 to 3 hours. Drain. Mix the remaining ingredients in a small saucepan. Bring them to a boil, remove from the heat, and pour over the cucumbers and onions. Stir to mix all the ingredients. Cover and refrigerate for 3 days, stirring occasionally.

NOTE: How about zucchini and summer squash pickles? Keith Hutchins, our gardening expert at the farm, had a surplus of zucchini and summer squash in his garden. (This shouldn't happen to an expert, should it?) He solved his problem by using this recipe to pickle them. They were delicious. He cut the squash into 2-inch chunks, added a dash of cinnamon to the brine, and then cooked the squash in the boiling brine for 1 minute. He refrigerated them for 3 days, and we all had squash pickles with lunch.

Raw Carrot Relish

This relish is made with raw vegetables and a hot marinade. But even though the vegetables marinate for 24 hours or longer, they are still crisp.

4 cups peeled, coarsely shredded
   carrots (about 1 pound)
²/₃ cup chopped red onion
³/₄ cup ¹/₄-inch diced green
   pepper
¹/₂ cup water
²/₃ cup sugar

²/₃ cup white vinegar
¹/₂ teaspoon salt
1 teaspoon whole cloves
1 teaspoon whole allspice
¹/₂ cinnamon stick

Mix the carrots, onion, and pepper in a glass or stainless-steel bowl.

Place the remaining ingredients in a small saucepan and bring to a boil. Lower the heat and simmer, covered, for 10 to 12 minutes. Strain the hot marinade, then pour over the carrot mixture. Mix very well. Cover and marinate in the refrigerator for at least 24 hours, stirring occasionally. Serve chilled.

Vinaigrette Dressing

MAKES ³/₄ CUP

Use this dressing on such salad greens as Ruby, Salad Bowl, or Boston (loose-leaf or native) lettuce. I really like tarragon in salad dressing, but its use is optional. You may eliminate the tarragon or substitute another herb. If you plan to use the vinaigrette for Spinach Salad, do not include the tarragon or other strong-flavored herb, as they overpower the spinach flavor.

2 tablespoons wine vinegar
1/2 teaspoon Dijon mustard
1/4 teaspoon garlic powder (or
   1/2 teaspoon minced garlic)
1/4 teaspoon sugar
1/2 teaspoon salt

1/8 teaspoon pepper
1 tablespoon chopped fresh
   tarragon (1/2 teaspoon dried)
1/2 cup salad oil (or
   combination salad and olive
   oil)

Place the vinegar, mustard, garlic, sugar, salt, pepper, and tarragon in a small mixing bowl. Mix thoroughly with a wire whisk or fork, slowly adding the oil, until well blended. Toss with the salad greens just before serving, using just enough to coat the greens.

NOTE: For variety, increase the amount of sugar to 1/2 teaspoon and stir in 1/4 cup tomato juice.

🐄 Garlic-Flavored Croutons

MAKES ABOUT 2 CUPS

I always make croutons in the oven rather than in a frying pan on the stove. They may not be as evenly browned, but they taste just as good and I don't have to stand over the pan. I don't bother to remove the crusts from the bread, but the croutons look better when you do.

Preheat the oven to 400°F.

3 tablespoons butter or
   margarine
1 clove garlic

3 slices bread, white, dark, or
   combination

Place the butter in a small saucepan. Peel and crush the clove of garlic slightly. Add the garlic to the butter and place the pan over low heat. When the butter has melted, remove the pan from the heat and let it rest for 5 minutes while the butter absorbs the garlic flavor. Remove the garlic and brush both sides of each slice of bread with butter. Stack the bread and cut it into 1/2- to 3/4-inch cubes. Place the cubes on a cookie sheet in a single layer and bake at 400°F, stirring once or twice, until brown and crisp (8 to 10 minutes). If you don't plan to use the croutons right away, store them in an airtight container.

5

Vegetables

*O*vercooked *vegetables are* neither attractive nor appetizing. They lose their color, texture, and flavor. When they are cooked so little that they still taste raw, they are also unappealing. However you cook your vegetables, it is important that you buy the freshest available and prepare them carefully to preserve their flavor.

There are several ways to cook vegetables — steaming, blanching, sautéing, and baking. Steaming, which is very popular today, is a good method for many vegetables. You need a steamer or a deep pan with a rack that will hold the vegetables above the water. Bring the water in the steamer to a boil before adding the vegetables. Do not overload the steamer or the vegetables on the bottom layers will overcook. Cover the pot when steaming.

To blanch vegetables, bring salted water to a boil in a large pan, add the vegetables, and cook until done. After putting in the vegetables, cover the pot. When the water returns to a boil, remove the lid and continue to cook until the vegetables are done to your liking.

Vegetables that cook quickly are ideal to sauté. I frequently sauté cabbage, zucchini and summer squash, pea pods, sliced kohlrabi, parsnips, and purple-top turnips. Sauté the vegetables in oil or butter or a combination of both in a large frying or sauté pan. For sautéing, the oil should be hot but not smoking. If you use butter, it should be barely melted (not brown) before you add the vegetables.

It is possible to bake many vegetables, but potatoes and winter squash are the ones that come to mind.

Many vegetables are unexpectedly delicious raw, for example, parsnips, butternut squash, yellow and white turnip, zucchini and summer squash. All of these are good on raw vegetable and dip platters or grated to make a salad similar to Carrot Salad or Coleslaw. They also taste good in a tossed salad or grated across the top of a salad to add interest and color. Similarly, many vegetables that we eat raw are equally good cooked. Hot celery, radishes, cucumbers, and salad greens are excellent. As a matter of fact, I think chicory is far better cooked and served with butter and salt and pepper than raw in a salad.

The vegetable recipes in this chapter are for those that we grow on our farms in Lexington, Massachusetts, and Litchfield, New Hampshire. I have not included vegetables that are not harvested in large quantities in New England.

Asparagus

Asparagus is so delicious plain that I rarely add anything but butter and salt. I wash the asparagus and break off the tough part of the stalk. When you bend the stalk, it breaks naturally where it becomes tender. However, if you want to use more of the asparagus, cut off any white and peel the stalk thinly before cooking. Though this takes extra time, you can enjoy more of the asparagus. I cook asparagus either by steaming or in a pan of simmering, salted water. When I steam them, I don't put more than a double layer in the pan because the vegetables on the bottom would overcook before the top layers are done. More often, I bring salted water to a boil in a deep frying pan, add the asparagus (no more than two deep), and simmer, uncovered, until done. Each method takes 10 to 12 minutes. Asparagus may also be stir-fried.

LOCAL SEASON: End of April to early July

❦ Asparagus with Hollandaise Puff

This topping is simply blender Hollandaise with stiffly beaten egg whites folded in. Spread it over cooked asparagus and place them under the broiler until brown just before serving. This sauce is good on other vegetables, too.

2 pounds asparagus
3 egg yolks, at room
   temperature
1 tablespoon lemon juice
¼ teaspoon salt

Pinch cayenne pepper
½ cup butter
2 egg whites, stiffly beaten

Trim and cook the asparagus until tender. Drain and place in an oven-to-table shallow baking dish.

Put the egg yolks, lemon juice, salt, and cayenne pepper in a blender. Melt the butter in a small saucepan until bubbly but not brown. Blend the egg yolks, juice, salt, and pepper on low speed. When blended, still using low speed, very slowly pour the hot butter in a thin stream into the egg yolk mixture while the blender is running. After all the butter has been incorporated, continue to blend only until the sauce thickens (10 to 15 seconds). Fold the beaten egg whites into the Hollandaise and spread the mixture over the asparagus. Place under the broiler until brown and serve immediately.

NOTE: To make plain Hollandaise sauce, eliminate the egg whites and serve the sauce as soon as it thickens in the blender.

Beans

As a native of the South, I like the flavor of salt pork in green beans. But when I don't have salt pork on hand, I do the next best thing and put a slice of bacon in my beans. I then cook them in boiling, salted water. I steam them occasionally, but only when I intend to use them in combination with another vegetable and don't want the bacon flavor. The standard green bean is a bush bean. I prefer the larger, heartier-flavored pole beans such as Kentucky Wonders, whose flavor is quite different from that of bush beans. Though I often use vegetables in casseroles, I seldom use beans, because I think they are better simply cooked. The length of time to cook beans depends on their size and your taste. I like them crisp-tender, slightly crunchy but not raw, so I cook them 8 to 12 minutes, depending on their size and whether they are whole or snapped. Wax beans take the same amount of time. Pole beans take about 12 minutes.

LOCAL SEASON: End of June to end of September or frost

🌿Beans with Sour Cream and Tarragon Sauce

Tarragon Sauce may be used with other vegetables as well as chicken and fish. The slight tarragon flavor complements the beans. For this recipe I steam the beans whole for about 12 minutes.

$1\frac{1}{2}$ pounds green beans
$1\frac{1}{2}$ tablespoons butter or margarine
1 small clove garlic, minced ($\frac{1}{2}$ teaspoon)
2 tablespoons finely chopped onion
$\frac{1}{3}$ cup light cream or milk

1 tablespoon flour
$\frac{2}{3}$ cup sour cream
1 to 2 teaspoons chopped fresh tarragon or $\frac{1}{2}$ teaspoon dried (or to taste)
$\frac{1}{4}$ teaspoon salt
Freshly ground pepper

Wash the beans, remove the ends, snap, if desired, and cook them. While they are cooking, make the sauce.

Melt the butter in a medium frying pan. Add the garlic and onion and sauté over medium-low heat until soft but not brown. Remove from the heat.

Put the flour and cream in a small mixing bowl. Blend them with a fork or wire whisk. Stir in the sour cream, tarragon, salt, and pepper. Stir the mixture into the frying pan. Return to the heat and cook, stirring, until thick. When the beans are done, drain them well and place in a serving dish. Spoon the sauce over the beans.

Fresh Shell Beans

The shell beans we sell are properly called horticultural beans. The large pods, which are not edible, are mottled red and cream and the mature beans are also cream with dark red markings. When they cook, the shelled beans lose their red color and become pale beige.

I understand that they are often cooked with salt pork and molasses in Maine. I simply cover the shelled beans with water, add ½ teaspoon of salt and a piece of bacon, bring them to a boil, lower the heat, and simmer, covered, for 25 to 30 minutes. When the beans are soft, I take off the cover and continue to cook until the liquid cooks out a bit, being careful not to scorch the beans. They are easy to cook and delicious.

Frank Palumbo, a farmer from the next town who also grows shell beans, told me that his wife adds chopped celery, onion, and fresh tomato to their beans, the amount being a matter of personal taste. I tried her method, adding the tomato toward the end of the cooking time. It was excellent.

LOCAL SEASON: Mid-July through September

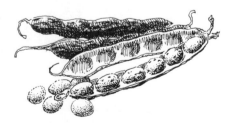

🌿 Baked Fresh Shell Beans

SERVES 6 TO 8

These taste like the baked beans made with dried beans except that the shell beans remain somewhat firmer.

Preheat the oven to 300°F.

4 cups beans (shelled)
¼ pound salt pork
4 cups water
1 cup coarsely chopped onion
⅓ cup molasses
⅓ cup lightly packed dark
  brown sugar

1 teaspoon dry mustard
1 teaspoon salt
⅛ teaspoon pepper
¼ cup ketchup

Put the shelled beans, salt pork (cut into 4 or 5 pieces), and water in a large pot. Bring to a boil, lower the heat, and simmer, covered, for 30 minutes. Remove from the heat. Do not drain.

Mix the remaining ingredients and stir them into the beans. Transfer the mixture to a 2-quart casserole. Cover and bake at 300°F for 1½ hours. Remove the cover and continue to bake for 30 minutes to 1 hour or until some of the liquid has been absorbed.

Beets

If you have a vegetable steamer, use it for beets. Steamed beets lose far less color than those cooked by other methods. Cut the stems to 1 inch above the beets (but don't cut the roots), and wash thoroughly, being careful not to damage the skin. Steam them (or cook in boiling water) for about 30 minutes for beets with a diameter of 2½ to 3 inches. Cut off the remaining stems, hold under cold, running water (so you won't burn your hands), and the skin just peels off. Slice the beets, add some butter, and serve. Add vinegar or lemon juice for a different flavor.

Beet Greens

I'm spoiled and seldom use the tops of my beets. They really are very good cooked, but we sell the small beet greens (thinnings), which are tastier by far, at the farm stand. I wash them in several changes of water, blanch them in boiling, salted water until they soften (3 to 4 minutes), drain them well, and serve them with butter. I don't use garlic or onion with beet greens, saving them for stronger-flavored greens.

LOCAL SEASON: Beets — early June through October.
                      Beet thinnings — mid-May through September

❧ Beets with Beet Purée

SERVES 4 TO 6

I like this dish for its double beet taste. Cooked sliced beets are served in a spicy puréed beet sauce.

6 to 8 beets (2- to 3-inch
diameter), cooked, peeled,
and sliced
3 tablespoons beet cooking
water
3 tablespoons red wine
vinegar
3 tablespoons sugar

1 tablespoon butter or
margarine, softened
2 tablespoons minced onion
1/4 teaspoon salt
1/8 teaspoon ground cloves

Cook the beets and peel and cut them into 1/4-inch slices, reserving the largest beet for the purée. Set aside.

Cut the reserved beet into chunks. Place the beet chunks in a blender or food processor with the remaining ingredients. If you forget to reserve the cooking water, use plain water. Purée. Put the sliced beets and purée in a saucepan and simmer, stirring often, for 5 to 10 minutes.

❧ Diced Beets in Light Vinegar Sauce

SERVES 3 TO 4

6 beets (2- to 2 1/2-inch diameter)
2 tablespoons butter or
margarine
3 tablespoons red wine vinegar

1 teaspoon sugar
1 tablespoon minced onion
1 teaspoon Worcestershire sauce
1/4 teaspoon salt

Cook, peel, and dice the beets. Set aside and make the sauce.

Put the remaining ingredients in a small saucepan. Bring to a simmer over low heat. Simmer for 3 to 4 minutes. Add the diced beets and stir to coat with the sauce. Heat gently before serving.

Broccoli

Broccoli is a versatile and popular vegetable. When I give farm tours to children, broccoli gets the largest show of hands when I ask, "Who likes this vegetable?" It is delicious raw in salad, great with chicken or beef in a casserole, ideal in quiche or soup, and especially good with pasta and cheese sauce. There's nothing worse than overcooked broccoli, so watch it carefully. I trim my broccoli, separate it into the size pieces I want, and wash it thoroughly. Either steam it or blanch it in boiling, salted water, uncovered, until the stems are fork-tender. When blanching, cook 5 to 7 minutes, depending on the size of the pieces. Steaming takes 2 to 3 minutes longer. Serve hot with butter, salt, and pepper.

LOCAL SEASON: Broccoli, a cool-weather crop, has two seasons — early June through mid-July and early September to late October.

🍃 Broccoli and Shells

SERVES 6 TO 8

The only drawback to this recipe is that it has to be put together at the last minute. Although it's nice as a first course or a luncheon dish, I usually serve it as a side dish for dinner when we're having plain meat such as broiled chicken or steak.

¾ cup heavy cream
2 eggs, beaten
⅔ cup grated Parmesan cheese
½ teaspoon salt
⅛ teaspoon freshly ground pepper
¾ pound broccoli (4 to 5 cups small florets)

3 cups medium shells
2 tablespoons butter or margarine
1 cup sliced mushrooms
1 clove garlic, minced

Mix the cream, eggs, cheese, salt, and pepper and set aside to come to room temperature.

Wash and trim the broccoli. Cut it into small florets and cook in boiling, salted water or steam until the broccoli is crisp-tender (not too soft).

Cook the shells as directed on the package until done to your taste. While the shells are cooking, melt the butter in a large frying pan. Add the mushrooms and garlic and sauté until soft but not brown. Add the broccoli and sauté for 1 minute. Remove from the heat. Drain the shells very well. Return them to the pot and stir in the broccoli-mushroom and the cream mixtures. The heat from the shells and broccoli will cook the cream and eggs. Serve immediately.

NOTE: You may substitute 1½ cups of elbow macaroni or 5 cups (½ pound) of wide egg noodles for the shells.

Brussels Sprouts

When you buy these miniature cabbages, pick out firm, compact sprouts with no yellow leaves. It's hard to say how long to cook Brussels sprouts because the size varies. Trim and wash them before cooking. Cut an X in the stem end so they will cook more quickly. Blanch them in boiling, salted water for 8 to 10 minutes or steam them 10 to 12 minutes. Overcooked Brussels sprouts lose their flavor, so watch them carefully. Serve Brussels sprouts with butter, cream sauce, or cheese sauce, or try one of the following recipes.

LOCAL SEASON: Early September through October

🌿 Brussels Sprouts Almandine

SERVES 3 TO 4

1 pound Brussels sprouts
3 tablespoons butter or
  margarine

⅓ cup blanched, slivered
  almonds

Wash, trim, and cook the Brussels sprouts. Drain the sprouts and cut them in half.

Melt the butter in a large frying pan and add the almonds. Sauté the almonds over medium heat until they are lightly browned. Add the Brussels sprout halves and sauté with the almonds for about 1 minute.

🌿 Brussels Sprouts with Tomato and Onion

SERVES 3 TO 4

¾ pound small Brussels
  sprouts
2 tablespoons butter or
  margarine
½ cup coarsely chopped onion
1½ cups peeled tomato (seeded,
  if desired)

½ teaspoon salt
⅛ teaspoon pepper
1 tablespoon grated Parmesan
  cheese (optional)

Steam the Brussels sprouts until tender. Remove from the heat and cut each sprout in half.

Melt the butter in a 2-quart saucepan. Add the onion and cook until soft. Add the tomatoes, sprouts, salt, and pepper. Cook for 2 to 3 minutes over medium heat or until the tomatoes are heated through. Sprinkle with Parmesan cheese.

Cabbage

Cabbage takes very little time to cook or prepare, so I serve it often. One of my favorite methods for green cabbage is to slice it thinly, as for cole slaw, then sauté or stir-fry it in a little butter until it is not quite limp. Use your imagination to vary the vegetable. For example, you could add peeled and chopped fresh tomatoes, curry powder, or finely chopped dill or tarragon. When you want wedges or large pieces of cabbage, steam or blanch them. Wedges cooked by either method take up to 10 minutes, depending on size, while pieces take only 3 to 5 minutes. I believe that many people claim to dislike cabbage because it's been overcooked, so don't cook it too long. It should remain a bit crisp. Red cabbage takes slightly longer to cook than green; Savoy cabbage takes about the same amount of time as green, and Chinese cabbage takes somewhat less time.

LOCAL SEASON: Green — early June through November
                 Red — mid-June through November

🌺 Sweet-and-Sour Red and Green Cabbage

SERVES 6

4 slices bacon, crisply cooked
   and crumbled
1½ tablespoons bacon fat
   (reserved from bacon)
1 tablespoon butter or
   margarine
½ cup chopped onion
2½ cups thinly sliced red
   cabbage

5 cups thinly sliced green
   cabbage
1 teaspoon salt
1 tablespoon dark brown sugar
1 tablespoon cider vinegar
½ teaspoon allspice
½ teaspoon dry mustard

Cook the bacon in a large frying pan until crisp, drain, and set aside. Pour out all but 1½ tablespoons of the fat. Add the butter, onion, and red cabbage to the fat and sauté over medium-low heat, stirring, until the onion begins to soften (about 1 minute). Add the green cabbage and salt, and continue to cook for 2 to 3 minutes, stirring often, until the cabbage is limp but not brown. (It cooks down very quickly.) The cabbage tastes very good at this point, but to make it sweet and sour, add the brown sugar, vinegar, allspice, and mustard. Stir over low heat until well blended. Stir in the bacon and serve immediately.

Carrots

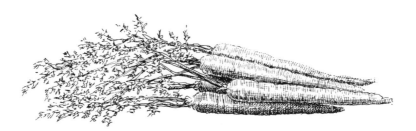

Carrots are one of the versatile root vegetables. Cooked, mashed carrot may be substituted for pumpkin or squash in bread or pie recipes. Carrots are good raw in cake or salad.

When I have small carrots, I peel them and cook them whole. I cut larger ones into pennies (rounds) or sticks before cooking. Carrots may be steamed — see Honey-Glazed Parsnip (or Carrot) Sticks, page 157 — or blanched. Carrot pennies or sticks cook in 4 to 6 minutes, depending on the size you cut. Try cooked shredded carrots. They can be steamed in 3 or 4 minutes. You may then serve them plain or, after steaming, place them in a frying pan with a little butter, a teaspoon or two of sugar, and a dash of cinnamon. Sauté them until the flavors are blended and serve. They are a pleasant change from ordinary cooked carrots.

Carrots can also be baked in the oven, as in the following recipe, Baked Carrot Sticks.

LOCAL SEASON: July 1 through early December. Carrots are sweetest in the fall when it is cool.

🌿Baked Carrot Sticks

SERVES 6

Preheat the oven to 350°F.

2 pounds carrots, peeled and cut
  into sticks
1 teaspoon salt
1 teaspoon sugar

Freshly ground pepper or
  Dash cinnamon
3 tablespoons butter or
  margarine

Place the carrots in a shallow 2-quart baking dish. Sprinkle them with the salt, sugar, and either pepper *or* cinnamon. Stir to mix. Dot with butter. Cover tightly with foil. Bake at 350°F for 45 to 50 minutes or until done. Stir once halfway through the baking period.

NOTE: You may also bake carrots at 400°F for 40 to 45 minutes.

Cauliflower

A whole head of cauliflower served on a plate is a beautiful presentation for a dinner party. You can top it with buttered bread crumbs or serve it with cheese sauce on the side. It takes 20 to 25 minutes to steam a whole head and 15 to 20 minutes to blanch one. For family meals, I prefer to break the cauliflower into small pieces (florets), wash them, and steam (6 to 8 minutes) or blanch (5 minutes) them and serve with butter, salt, and pepper.

LOCAL SEASON: Cauliflower, a cool-weather crop, has two seasons — early to late June and early September to late October.

🌿 Cauliflower and Mushrooms with Cheese Sauce

SERVES 6 TO 8

I've added mushrooms to my favorite cauliflower with cheese sauce recipe and put it in a casserole. It can be made ahead of time and baked just before dinner.

Preheat the oven to 375°F. Butter a shallow 1½-quart casserole.

1½ pound head cauliflower
  (medium)
1½ cups thickly sliced
  mushrooms
  4 tablespoons butter or
  margarine
  3 tablespoons flour
1½ cups milk

½ teaspoon salt
⅛ teaspoon pepper
¼ teaspoon dry mustard
1½ to 2 cups shredded medium
  sharp cheddar cheese
  2 tablespoons grated
  Parmesan cheese

Break the cauliflower into florets, wash them, and cook in boiling, salted water or steam until crisp-tender. Drain well.

Place 1 tablespoon of the butter in a frying pan over medium heat. Add the sliced mushrooms and sauté for 2 or 3 minutes or until soft. Set the mushrooms aside and make the cheese sauce.

Melt the remaining 3 tablespoons of butter in a 3-quart saucepan over medium heat. Stir in the flour and cook for 1 minute or until smooth. Stir in the milk and continue to cook, stirring, until the mixture thickens and boils. Stir in the salt, pepper, mustard, and cheddar cheese. Cook, stirring, until the cheese melts and the sauce is smooth. Remove from the heat. Add the sautéed mushrooms and cauliflower. Stir until well mixed and turn into the prepared casserole. Sprinkle the top with Parmesan cheese. Bake at 375°F for 20 to 30 minutes or until the sauce is bubbly and the top is lightly browned.

Celery

I use celery many ways, stir-frying it with other vegetables, in stuffing, and, of course, raw in salads. I prefer to stir-fry it, but poaching it in liquid (broth is best) is the other way I cook it. I remove only the strings from the outer stalks if it seems necessary. Celery is a member of the parsley family, so its leaves are good for flavoring soups.

LOCAL SEASON: Late July to mid-October

✿ Baked Celery and Almonds

SERVES 4

How about a celery casserole? For someone like me, who absolutely despises braised celery, the idea sounds dreadful. However, this dish is so good that I serve it to guests.

Preheat the oven to 350°F.

3 tablespoons butter or margarine
3½ cups ¼-inch slices celery
⅓ cup blanched, slivered almonds
1⅓ cups chopped mushrooms
1 clove garlic, peeled
4 tablespoons flour

¾ cup Chicken Broth (recipe, page 40)
1 cup light cream
½ teaspoon salt
Pepper to taste
2 tablespoons grated Parmesan cheese (optional)

Melt 2 tablespoons of the butter in a large frying pan. Add the celery, almonds, mushrooms, and garlic. Cook over medium heat, stirring often, until the celery starts to soften (8 to 10 minutes). Remove from the heat and discard the garlic. Remove the vegetables from the pan with a slotted spoon, leaving the drippings, and transfer to a 1-quart casserole.

Measure the flour and broth into a mixing bowl. Using a wire whisk or fork, mix them until smooth. Add the cream and stir to blend.

Return the frying pan to the heat and add the remaining 1 tablespoon of butter. When the butter has melted, add the flour-broth-cream mixture. Cook over medium heat, stirring, until the mixture thickens and boils. Cook for 1 minute and remove from the heat. Add the salt and pepper to taste. Pour the sauce over the vegetables in the casserole. Sprinkle the top with cheese. Bake at 350°F for 30 to 35 minutes.

Corn

Sweet corn is the mainstay of most New England farmstands. Ours is no exception, and we often have a long line at our corn table. Our customers know that corn is best when just picked, so we see the same faces day after day. It is important that you buy only the amount of corn you need each time. Even refrigerated, corn loses flavor rapidly after it is picked. If you aren't going to use it immediately, refrigerate it unhusked, and use it as soon as possible.

Corn on the cob is a summer staple at our house, and I serve it either at lunch or dinner almost every day during the season. I shuck it, put it into boiling water (no salt or sugar), and cook it for just 4 minutes after the water returns to a boil. Although many of our customers disagree, my personal preference is for young, light ears when I cook corn on the cob or sautéed corn. I use heavier, more mature, corn when I make corn chowder.

Years ago, the corn season ended around the beginning of September. Today, however, there are several later varieties, and excellent sweet corn is usually available until the first heavy frost. Although yellow corn is not as popular as the bicolored varieties in our area, we still have customers who prefer it, and I find that many varieties are just as sweet as the two-tone. We also grow a small amount of the very sweet white corn, which is delicious. For a change, I occasionally cut the corn off the cob with a very sharp knife and simply stir-fry the kernels in butter for 2 or 3 minutes.

LOCAL SEASON: Mid-July to early October or frost.

🌿 Stir-Fried Corn

Corn off the cob is just as delicious, and a lot less messy to eat, as corn on the cob.

7 to 8 ears corn	¼ cup chopped green pepper
3 tablespoons butter or margarine	½ cup peeled, seeded, chopped tomato
⅓ cup chopped onion	Salt and pepper to taste

Cut the kernels off the cobs with a sharp knife. You should have approximately 4 cups.

Melt the butter in a large frying pan over medium heat. Add the onion and pepper and cook until soft but not brown. Add the corn kernels and cook for 3 to 4 minutes. Stir in the tomato and cook for 1 to 2 minutes longer or until the tomato is hot. Serve immediately.

Cucumbers

Cucumbers are among the neglected vegetables often relegated to salads. Unfortunately, they are seldom served hot. Peeled, seeded, and sliced or cut into chunks, they are marvelous sautéed in a little butter or oil and sprinkled with a chopped herb (dill is traditional with cucumbers). Don't overcook them, as they taste best with some texture left. When I cook cucumbers, I use the standard variety, not the long, burpless or the pickling type, which I use for salads. During the winter, when cucumbers are shipped into our area, I find that the pickling cucumbers have the best flavor in salad.

LOCAL SEASON: Mid-June through September

✿ Cucumbers and Tomatoes

SERVES 4

3 cucumbers (about 1½
   pounds total)
2½ tablespoons butter or
   margarine
½ cup coarsely chopped
   onion
1½ to 2 cups peeled and
   chopped tomatoes
   (seeded, if desired)

1½ tablespoons chopped fresh
   basil or 1 teaspoon dried
Salt and pepper to taste

Peel the cucumbers, remove the seeds, and cut into ½-inch chunks.

Melt the butter in a large frying pan. Add the onion and sauté until soft (about 1 minute). Add the cucumber chunks and cook, stirring often, for 5 to 6 minutes or until they soften. Add the tomatoes, basil, and salt and pepper. Cook gently only until the tomatoes are heated through and the flavors blended. If the dish seems watery, thicken it with a few fresh bread crumbs.

NOTE: Don't overcook the cucumbers. They should retain their shape and some texture.

Eggplant

There are so many ways to use eggplant: fried, stuffed, ratatouille, moussaka, and so forth. Fried is the most popular at our house. I don't deep-fry it, so I should really call it sautéed or pan-fried. I also bake unpeeled ½-inch slices of eggplant. Brush the slices on both sides with oil, sprinkle them with salt, place them on a cookie sheet, and bake at 400°F for 10 minutes or until the slices are soft. Then top each slice with a thin slice of tomato and grated Parmesan cheese and place them under the broiler until the cheese browns. If I'm out of tomato, I use buttered bread crumbs or sliced cheese. This is attractive and makes an easy, quick vegetable dish.

LOCAL SEASON: Mid-July through September

Eggplant Casserole

SERVES 4 TO 6

Eggplant is most often served with tomato, so I guess that's why I like this recipe so much — no tomato.

Preheat the oven to 350°F. Butter a shallow 1½-quart casserole.

4 cups peeled, diced eggplant (1 1-pound eggplant)	2 eggs, beaten
5½ tablespoons butter or margarine	¼ teaspoon salt Dash cayenne pepper
6 ounces cream cheese, softened	⅓ cup dry bread crumbs Dash garlic powder
¾ cup milk	

Peel the eggplant and cut it into ⅓- to ½-inch cubes. Melt 4 tablespoons of the butter in a large frying pan. Add the eggplant and sauté until it softens (5 to 6 minutes). Set aside. Place the cream cheese in a mixing bowl and beat it with a spoon or an electric mixer until smooth.

Scald the milk, then slowly beat it into the cream cheese. When beaten smooth, stir in the eggs, salt, cayenne pepper, and eggplant. Spoon the mixture into the prepared casserole. Bake at 350°F for 15 minutes.

While the casserole is baking, melt the remaining 1½ tablespoons of butter and stir in the bread crumbs and garlic powder. After 15 minutes, sprinkle the buttered bread crumbs over the top of the casserole and continue to bake for 10 to 15 minutes longer. Remove the casserole from the oven and let it rest for 5 to 10 minutes before serving. If necessary place it under the broiler to brown the crumbs.

🌿 *Fried Eggplant or Zucchini*

SERVES 3 TO 4

These vegetables are a favorite not only at home. When I arrived at the farm with a plateful of each, the greenhouse crew was potting chrysanthemums. They just wiped off their dirty hands and snitched samples as I walked by. I slice the eggplant straight across in rounds, but I slice the zucchini on a diagonal to get ovals. The zucchini may also be cut into sticks (larger than carrot sticks — about ½ inch) before frying. They go well as hors d'oeuvres with a sauce.

1½ *pounds eggplant or*	¼ *teaspoon pepper*
1½ to 2 *pounds zucchini*	¼ *teaspoon dried oregano*
(2 medium)	¼ *teaspoon dried basil*
2 *eggs, slightly beaten*	½ *cup grated Parmesan cheese*
1 *tablespoon water*	*(optional)*
¾ *cup bread crumbs*	3 *tablespoons oil*
¾ *teaspoon salt*	

Peel and slice the eggplant into ⅓-inch slices. When you use zucchini, don't peel it, but slice it ¼-inch thick.

Mix the eggs and water thoroughly in a shallow pan. (A pie plate or layer cake pan works well.) Mix the crumbs, salt, pepper, oregano, basil, and cheese in another shallow pan. Heat the oil over medium heat in a large frying pan. Dip the vegetable slices first in the egg, coating both sides, then in the crumb mixture, again coating both sides. Fry in hot oil, turning once, until both sides are brown and the vegetable is soft. Serve with meat.

Greens

At our house, we can't agree on the greens we prefer. I think kale is terrific, but I'm afraid I'm the only one who feels that way. Everyone likes both red and green Swiss chard, beet greens, spinach, and cooked chicory and escarole. Dandelions are Alan's favorite, but the season is very short.

All greens should be washed thoroughly. I let the greens soak in lukewarm water for a few minutes, then lift them out into fresh water and continue washing in clean water until all the dirt is removed. I use cold water when I'm washing greens to use raw in salads.

I just wilt spinach with the water that remains on the leaves after washing. I blanch other greens in boiling, salted water until just tender. The time required to cook greens varies from 3 to 4 minutes for small beet greens to 8 to 10 minutes for kale.

Swiss chard is really a separate vegetable. After washing it, I slice the stalks across in ½-inch slices and add them to the leaves to cook. The combined sliced stalks and leaves cook in about 5 minutes in boiling water. When you cut the stalks into larger pieces, the greens are done long before the stalks. We occasionally sell small Swiss chard (thinnings, like beet greens). These take only 3 to 4 minutes to cook.

Cooked greens may be served with butter, salt, and pepper or chopped and sautéed with oil and garlic for a minute or two.

LOCAL SEASON: Kale — early June to December (the late kale is
                 better)
                 Swiss Chard — early June through October
                 Beet Greens — mid-May through September
                 Spinach: two seasons — mid-May to mid-June; late
                 August to December
                 Chicory, Escarole — mid-June through October

🌿 Escarole Sautéed with Garlic

SERVES 4 TO 6

One night, when we were having dinner in the North End (the Italian section) of Boston, sautéed escarole with garlic was listed under appetizers. I tried it and thought it was wonderful. I don't serve it as a first course, but we do have it often as a vegetable dish. So, all you garlic lovers, here's a recipe for you. Use coarsely chopped garlic — as much or as little as you like. You can cook any greens — for example, chicory and spinach — the same way.

2 pounds escarole
2 tablespoons olive oil
2 tablespoons vegetable oil

½ cup chopped onions
1 tablespoon coarsely chopped garlic (2 large cloves)

Trim the escarole and wash it thoroughly. Cook it in boiling, salted water until tender (about 5 minutes). Drain and chop. Don't squeeze dry, just drain well. You should have 2½ to 3 cups of chopped escarole.

Put the two kinds of oil in a large frying pan over medium-low heat. When the oil is warm, add the onions and garlic and sauté until soft. Don't brown. Stir in the chopped escarole and continue to cook for 3 to 4 minutes or until the flavors are well blended. Add salt, if necessary.

Kohlrabi

Kohlrabi is an old-fashioned vegetable that has recently become fashionable. Why it ever fell out of favor I don't understand, because it is excellent raw or cooked. Kohlrabi is odd-looking, resembling a spacecraft. It's a familiar vegetable in Asia, where it is used in Oriental cooking.

Kohlrabi is good raw with a dip or in a grated salad like Coleslaw or in place of parsnips in parsnip salad. It can also be cooked and diced, then made into a salad similar to Potato Salad. The bulbs may be steamed, but I generally peel them, cover them with water, add salt, and boil them until tender (20 to 30 minutes). They may then be served whole, or large ones sliced, with butter or sauce or diced for salad.

Don't ignore the greens if they look fresh. Kohlrabi greens are milder than turnip or collard greens. Wash them thoroughly after removing the stems and heavy ribs. Blanch the greens in boiling, salted water until tender (8 to 10 minutes), drain, and chop. Serve with butter or sauté in oil and garlic briefly before serving. Kohlrabi bulbs may also be peeled and chopped into ½-inch pieces and then cooked with the greens.

LOCAL SEASON: Early June through October

🌿 Sautéed Kohlrabi and Leeks

SERVES 4

Sauté small kohlrabi. Large ones should be cooked in boiling water.

1 pound leeks (3 to 4 medium)	*4 tablespoons butter or*
8 kohlrabi (1½- to 2-inch	*margarine*
diameter)	*Salt and pepper to taste*

Trim the roots and dark green leaves from the leeks, leaving the white and light green. Split the leeks lengthwise and wash to remove sand. Slice crosswise thinly into ⅛-inch pieces. Peel and slice the kohlrabi thinly. Melt the butter in a large frying pan. Add the kohlrabi slices and sauté for 2 to 3 minutes. Add the leeks and sauté, stirring, until the kohlrabi has begun to soften and the leeks are lightly browned. Season to taste.

Leeks

Since we started raising leeks, I find that I use them more and
more. The flavor is milder than that of onions, so if I substitute
leeks for onions in soups or other dishes I use about one-third
more leeks than onions. (If the recipe calls for ⅔ cup onions, use
1 cup leeks.) They are excellent sautéed with vegetables or served
by themselves. It is necessary to wash leeks thoroughly, as they
tend to hold dirt. Cut off the roots and dark green leaves down to
the pale green section. Even if you want to cook them whole, split
the leeks halfway down into the white and wash under running
water. Leeks may be steamed, but I find the texture is best when
they are simmered in water or broth, which I prefer, until done.
The time varies with the size of the leeks. Medium leeks are done
in 10 to 12 minutes. Whole leeks can be served with butter, hot
vinaigrette sauce, cream sauce, cheese sauce, and in many other
ways.

LOCAL SEASON: Early August to late December

🍃 Leeks in Mornay Sauce

SERVES 6

When I made this dish to check the quantities, I naturally took it to the farm for comments. I was amazed at how many of our employees had never eaten leeks. One girl told me that before she worked at the farm, she didn't know what they were. Everyone seemed to enjoy them, so I am encouraged to try more leek recipes in the future. I think the small amount of wine in this recipe adds a lovely flavor. However, if you prefer not to use it, simply increase the amount of chicken broth to 2⅓ cups.

Butter a shallow 1½-quart casserole.

8 to 10 medium leeks	*¼ cup flour*
2 cups Chicken Broth (recipe, page 40)	*2 tablespoons heavy cream*
	Salt and pepper to taste
⅓ cup dry white wine (vermouth is fine)	*1⅓ cup shredded Swiss cheese*
3 tablespoons butter or margarine	

Wash the leeks carefully. Cut the white part only into ¾- to 1-inch lengths (4 to 5 cups cut leeks). Place the broth and wine in a 3-quart saucepan. Bring to a boil and add the leek pieces. Lower the heat and simmer, covered, until the leeks are tender (10 to 12 minutes). Remove the leeks with a slotted spoon to the prepared casserole, reserving the liquid.

Melt the butter in a 2-quart saucepan over medium heat. Add the flour and cook for 1 to 2 minutes. Stir in the wine and broth mixture and the cream. Cook, stirring, until the mixture thickens and boils. Add 1 cup of the Swiss cheese and stir until the cheese melts. Remove from the heat and pour over the leeks. Sprinkle the remaining cheese over the top. Before serving, place the dish under the broiler until the cheese browns and the sauce bubbles.

Onions

There are many types of onions: chives, scallions, shallots, garlic, yellow, white, and red onions, sweet Spanish onions, and leeks. They are used for flavor in cooking around the world in unlimited ways. They are probably the most valuable vegetables in my kitchen.

I use plain yellow onions most often. Raw red and Spanish onions are good in salads or sliced for sandwiches. The sweet Spanish onions are also excellent for sautéing or for deep-frying.

Scallions are often included in stir-fried dishes and are also delicious raw in salads. A small amount of finely chopped shallots (or garlic) cooked until soft (not brown) in a little butter makes a delicious butter sauce with vegetables, meat, or fish. Swordfish or steak are especially good with this flavored butter. White onions are traditional for Thanksgiving dinner in many homes, and ours is no exception. I serve them either buttered or creamed.

LOCAL SEASON: Scallions — early June through October
       Onions — August through October

🌿 Creamed White Onions

SERVES 6 TO 8

2 pounds peeled white onions (about 24)
4 tablespoons butter or margarine
4 tablespoons flour
1 cup milk

¾ cup light cream
½ teaspoon salt
  Pepper to taste
1 tablespoon sherry (optional)

Cook the onions in boiling, salted water until tender (about 20 minutes). Drain well.

While the onions are cooking, make the cream sauce. Melt the butter in a 2-quart saucepan over low heat. Stir in the flour and cook, stirring, for 1 minute. Remove from the heat and stir in the milk and cream. Return to the heat and bring to a boil, stirring. Lower the heat and simmer for 3 to 5 minutes. Stir in the salt, pepper, and sherry.

Pour the sauce over the drained onions.

NOTE: If you would like to serve them from a casserole, place the cooked, drained onions in a shallow 1½-quart casserole. Pour the sauce over the onions. Sprinkle ½ cup of shredded Swiss cheese and 1 tablespoon of grated Parmesan cheese over the top. Bake the casserole at 400°F for 20 minutes or until the cheese melts and browns and the sauce is bubbly.

Parsnips

Parsnips are a vegetable ignored by too many people. They are super just boiled or steamed and mashed with butter, salt, and pepper. Like carrots and winter squash, they are delicious in breads and desserts, and they can be shredded and used raw in salads. They are naturally sweet and even more so when wintered over and dug in the spring.

I peel parsnips, cut them into chunks or sticks, cover them with water in a saucepan, add salt (½ to 1 teaspoon, depending on the amount of parsnips), cover them, and bring the water to a boil. I then lower the heat and simmer until the pieces are fork-tender (about 10 minutes) and drain. Steamed parsnips take a few minutes longer. When I serve parsnips as a vegetable, I whip the chunks with my electric mixer or mash them and add butter, salt, and pepper to taste. When I cook parsnips for muffins or pie, I don't put salt in the water, but I cook them the same way and whip or mash them until smooth.

I often sauté thinly sliced parsnips (or halved parboiled ones) in butter over medium heat until they're tender and brown. If the parsnip slices don't soften enough, cover the pan for a minute or two and let them steam until soft.

LOCAL SEASON: Two seasons — early March through April (wintered over); early September through February

Grated Parsnip Patties

MAKES 8 TO 10 PATTIES

Parsnip patties are similar to potato pancakes and should be served as a vegetable. You may serve them with sour cream, but they are very good plain.

3 cups peeled, grated parsnip
  (about ¾ pound)

2 tablespoons finely chopped
  onion

2 eggs, beaten
1/3 cup flour
1 tablespoon butter or
    margarine, melted
1/4 cup milk

1/2 teaspoon salt
1/8 teaspoon freshly ground
    pepper
1 to 2 tablespoons oil or solid
    shortening

Mix all the ingredients, with the exception of the oil, in a large bowl.

Place a small amount of oil (1 to 2 tablespoons) in a large frying pan over medium heat. When the oil is hot, drop the parsnip mixture into the pan by spoonfuls. Flatten them into 2-inch patties with the back of the spoon.

Fry, turning once, until the patties are brown on both sides — about 5 minutes per side.

NOTE: When you place them in the frying pan, the patties will appear to be dry and uneven. However, the mixture adheres as they fry.

Honey-Glazed Parsnip (or Carrot) Sticks

SERVES 6

Parsnip haters will enjoy them this way because they are sweet. When I served them at the farm stand, most people didn't know what they were eating. The carrot sticks are equally good.

1 1/2 pounds parsnips or carrots
2 tablespoons butter
3 tablespoons honey

1/4 teaspoon cinnamon (more to
    taste)

Peel the parsnips and cut them into 2-inch sticks (logs). Cook the sticks in boiling, salted water or steam for 5 to 10 minutes until almost tender. Don't overcook, since they will cook more in the glaze. Drain. At this point you may refrigerate the sticks and glaze them just before serving.

Place the butter, honey, and cinnamon in a large frying pan. Melt them over medium heat and add the parsnips. Sauté the sticks, stirring often, until the liquid is absorbed — 8 to 10 minutes. Serve immediately.

Peas

Peas are best (and sweetest) when picked, shelled, cooked in a minimum of water, seasoned with salt, pepper, and butter, and eaten immediately — or raw out of the pod. Like corn, peas seem to lose flavor rapidly once they are picked, so if you aren't going to use them right away, refrigerate them unshelled. When you are ready to cook the peas, shell them, place about 1 inch of water in the bottom of a saucepan (when you cook a large amount of peas, use a large saucepan), add ½ to 1 teaspoon of salt, depending on the quantity of peas, and bring the water to a boil. Add the peas and return the water to a boil. Lower the heat and cook, uncovered, for 4 to 5 minutes. Drain, add butter, if desired, and serve. You can stir in a touch of chopped fresh mint, some sautéed mushrooms, or toasted pine nuts or almonds if you like. However, if you are bored with plain peas, you can always add raw ones to a tossed salad or cook them for pea salad or mix them with rice.

Sugar Snap Peas

We really like the sugar snap peas that now grow. You eat them pods and all, but they are very different from snow peas, since there are large peas inside the edible pods. It's great not to have to shell them, but they do have to be strung on both sides. I serve them either raw with a dip or sauté them briefly in butter, sprinkle with salt, and serve. They really should be sautéed for 2 or 3 minutes or only until they are heated through. Overcooked peas lose their color and texture.

Snow Peas

For quick preparation, I stir-fry (sauté) snow peas with sliced mushrooms in a little butter or oil. The stem tips have to be removed before cooking. Snow peas take a minute or two longer than sugar snaps to cook. Add soy sauce instead of salt and a sprinkling of chopped or ground ginger for an Oriental taste.

LOCAL SEASON: Peas — mid-June to mid-July
Sugar snaps — end of June to end of July
Snow peas — mid-June through August

🌿 *Peas and Rice*

SERVES 6

4 tablespoons butter or
  margarine
⅓ cup chopped onion
1 small clove garlic, minced
¾ cup uncooked rice
1½ cups water (see note below)

1 teaspoon salt
1½ cups coarsely chopped
  mushrooms (sliced if small)
1½ cups fresh shelled peas
Salt and pepper to taste

Melt 2 tablespoons of the butter in a 2-quart saucepan. Add the onion and garlic and sauté until soft but not brown. Add the rice and stir until coated with butter. Add the water and salt. Cover and bring to a boil over high heat. Stir, lower the heat, and simmer, covered, until the rice is done.

While the rice is cooking, sauté the mushrooms in the remaining 2 tablespoons of butter. Set aside, saving the mushrooms and any liquid or butter remaining in the pan.

Cook the peas in 1 inch of boiling, salted water until done (4 to 5 minutes). Drain them well and set aside. When the rice is ready, stir in the peas and mushrooms, season to taste, and serve.

NOTE: The necessary amount of water may vary with the type of rice you use. Check the instructions on the package. For a different taste, stir 1 to 2 teaspoons of chopped fresh mint into the peas.

Peppers

The familiar green and red peppers are sweet bell peppers. Surprisingly, they are also available in yellow, brown, and purple, but these are something of a novelty. When I have the odd colors, I usually use them in salads or on raw vegetable and dip platters, where they always receive attention. We also grow the sweet Italian peppers that are so good for sautéing.

I am particularly fond of red peppers and eat them raw as I do fruit. I use red peppers in cooking (and, of course, salads) because of their special flavor, but green peppers are almost as essential to me as onions. They are delicious raw in salads and cooked in many, many dishes. Peppers make excellent containers for stuffings and even for other vegetables. Blanched until tender and filled with corn kernels, they are very attractive on a plate. When peppers are too large to fill for one serving, cut them in half lengthwise and fill the pepper boats with cooked corn, carrots, or cauliflower. Any vegetable that offers a color contrast is good. Just be sure that the pepper containers have been cooked long enough to be tender.

LOCAL SEASON: Mid-July to early October

❧ Mixed Vegetables or Peppers, Onions, Tomatoes, and Zucchini

SERVES 4

I guess this should be called Italian-style vegetables. The proportions of the vegetables may be varied, and the result will still be good.

1½ tablespoons vegetable or olive oil

1 medium to large yellow onion, sliced (¼ to ½ pound)

1 large green pepper (2 small) in ¼-inch strips

1 pound zucchini (2 medium), sliced into thin rounds

½ teaspoon salt

1 tablespoon chopped fresh basil (½ teaspoon dried)

2 to 3 teaspoons chopped fresh oregano (½ teaspoon dried)

1½ to 2 cups peeled, chopped tomato (seeded, if desired)

3 tablespoons grated Parmesan cheese

Heat the oil in a frying pan. Add the onion and pepper and sauté until the onion is soft (3 to 4 minutes). Add the zucchini, salt, basil, and oregano and cook over low heat until the zucchini softens (4 to 5 minutes). Add the tomato and cook for 5 minutes longer or until the tomatoes cook down and the vegetables are done. Stir in the cheese.

Potatoes

Potatoes are universally popular and are one of the top-selling vegetables at our stand. We grow all-purpose boiling potatoes, russet (baking) potatoes, and red-skinned potatoes on our New Hampshire farm.

I probably prepare mashed potatoes more often than any other kind. I should call them whipped, because I beat them with my hand electric mixer until they are fluffy and smooth. I peel and cut all-purpose potatoes into chunks, cover them with water, add salt, and boil until tender. I drain them well, add butter and milk, and whip. When I make them for company or a holiday dinner, I use light cream instead of milk. A food processor doesn't do a good job of whipping potatoes. If you don't have a mixer, an old-fashioned potato masher is fine. I usually add freshly ground pepper (white, when available) to my whipped potatoes. The length of time to cook potatoes varies both with the type you use and the size you cut them into, but plan on 10 to 15 minutes.

When I boil small, red-skinned potatoes or other small, new potatoes, I don't bother to peel them. I wash them well, cover them with salted water, and boil them until tender (20 to 30 minutes for potatoes 2 inches in diameter). I generally put them on the table whole, to be eaten with butter, salt, and pepper. Leftovers make excellent Lyonnaise Potatoes. Small unpeeled potatoes are also good in potato salad.

I bake russet potatoes, and they are marvelous. The whole family eats their potato skins, so I scrub the potatoes well, pierce them a couple of times with a fork, and grease the skins before baking. It doesn't matter whether you use oil, shortening, or butter, but greasing seems to make the skin taste even better and stay a little softer. Russet potatoes take about an hour to bake at 400°F. If your potatoes are enormous, plan on extra baking time.

LOCAL SEASON: All-purpose — harvested mid-August to early
                October
                Red-skinned — harvested late July to early
                September
                Russet — harvested mid-September to mid-
                October
                Local potatoes, because they are stored, are
                available year round.

❧ *Potato Pancakes*

MAKES 8 TO 10 2-INCH PATTIES

These pancakes are not for breakfast, but rather patties to serve
with dinner. They are made with grated raw potatoes. Traditionally, they are served with sour cream or applesauce. However, they
taste fine just plain, too.

2 eggs
2 medium potatoes
*2 tablespoons finely chopped
   shallots*
2 tablespoons flour
³⁄₄ teaspoon salt

*¹⁄₈ teaspoon freshly ground
   pepper*
*2 tablespoons butter or
   margarine*
2 tablespoons salad oil

Beat the eggs in a mixing bowl. Peel the potatoes, grate them, and
squeeze them dry with your hands. You should have about 2 cups
of grated potatoes. Add the potatoes, shallots, flour, salt, and pepper to the eggs. Stir to mix.

Put the oil and butter in a large frying pan and place over medium
heat. When the oil and butter are hot, drop the potato mixture by
spoonfuls into the pan, shaping and flattening the pancakes with
the spoon. Cook, turning once, until they are brown on both sides
— about 4 minutes per side.

🌿 Creamy Scalloped Potatoes

Preheat the oven to 350°F. Butter a deep 2- or 2½-quart casserole.

⅓ cup finely chopped onion
1 small clove garlic, finely chopped
2½ to 3 pounds all-purpose potatoes
4 tablespoons flour
2 tablespoons butter

1½ teaspoons salt
¼ teaspoon freshly ground pepper
Nutmeg
2 cups light cream
1 cup milk

Mix the onion and garlic and set aside. Peel and slice the potatoes thinly. Place one-third of the potatoes in the prepared casserole. Sprinkle one-third of the combined onion and garlic, 1 tablespoon of the flour, ½ teaspoon salt, one-third of the pepper, and a dusting of nutmeg over the potatoes and dot with one-third of the butter. Repeat with the second third of the potatoes and one-third of the other ingredients, except for the flour, using 2 tablespoons of flour on the middle layer. Place the last third of the potatoes and remaining seasoning and butter in a third layer. Scald the cream and milk together and pour over the potatoes. Cover the casserole and bake at 350°F, covered, for 30 minutes. Uncover and continue to bake for 1 hour longer or until the potatoes are soft and the top is brown.

🌿 Red-Skinned Lyonnaise Potatoes

SERVES 3 TO 4

This is really more of a hint than a recipe. I usually cook a few extra potatoes so that I can make Lyonnaise Potatoes the next night.

5 to 6 small red-skinned
    potatoes, cooked
  3 tablespoons butter or
    margarine
  1 tablespoon salad oil

⅔ cup coarsely chopped onion
¼ teaspoon salt (or to taste)
⅛ teaspoon freshly ground
   pepper

Cut the cooked potatoes (cold or hot) into ¼-inch slices. Do not peel. Heat the butter and oil in a large frying pan over medium-high. Add the onions, potatoes, salt, and pepper, and sauté until the potatoes are lightly browned and the onions are cooked. Correct the seasoning.

Radishes

Radishes are generally served raw, sliced into salads or whole on a relish dish. No one has even served them to me cooked. When cooked, they lose their familiar hot, sharp flavor and develop a milder taste, similar to that of purple-top turnips. Steamed whole, radishes turn a lovely pink. Just remove the tops, wash the radishes, and steam for 9 to 12 minutes, depending on their size. They may then be served with butter, salt, and pepper or with a cheese or cream sauce. A recipe for sautéed radishes follows.

LOCAL SEASON: Early May through October

Sautéed Radishes

This dish is a lovely color combination. A small amount of chopped fresh basil, dill, or other herb makes a nice addition.

3 tablespoons butter or
   margarine
²/₃ cup ¹/₄-inch slices
   scallions
2 to 3 cups (unpeeled) sliced
   radishes
   2 cups 2- to 3-inch zucchini
   sticks

2 cups 2- to 3-inch summer
   squash sticks
¹/₂ teaspoon salt (or to taste)
¹/₈ teaspoon ground pepper

Melt the butter in a large frying pan over medium heat. Add the scallions and radishes and sauté for 1 minute. Add the zucchini, summer squash, salt, and pepper. Continue to sauté for 3 to 4 minutes longer or until the radishes are pink and the vegetables are crisp-tender.

NOTE: Cut the squash in 2- to 3-inch sticks like carrot sticks.

Spinach

Nothing tastes better than good fresh spinach — or worse than gritty fresh spinach. So make sure to spend the extra few minutes to wash it an additional time. People who have double sinks are in luck when they wash greens, because it is so easy to switch from one sink to the other. Even if you have only one sink, soak spinach (and other greens) in at least three waters. If the spinach is untrimmed, cut the roots and stems off before washing. When the spinach is well washed, put the wet spinach in a large pot. Place over low heat, cover, and wilt the spinach. The spinach will give off more than enough liquid to cook in. When wilted (less than 5 minutes), drain and chop. Add butter, salt, and pepper and serve. When you use spinach in other dishes, such as omelets or quiches, squeeze the spinach dry with your hands before chopping it.

LOCAL SEASON: Spinach, a cool-weather crop, has two seasons — mid-May to mid-June; late August to December.

❧ *Noodles with Spinach Sauce*

SERVES 6 TO 8

When you want a change from plain or creamed spinach, try this recipe. It tastes good with prosciutto or ham or without either.

2 pounds fresh spinach
  (1½ pounds trimmed)
6 ounces (or ⅓ pound)
  medium or wide egg noodles
3 tablespoons butter or
  margarine
⅓ cup chopped scallions
1 clove garlic, finely minced
  (1 teaspoon)

¼ pound prosciutto or cooked
  ham, finely chopped
  (optional)
3 tablespoons flour
2½ cups light cream
½ teaspoon salt (or to taste)
¼ cup grated Parmesan cheese
  (optional)

Trim and wash the spinach. Place the wet spinach in a large saucepan and wilt over medium heat (approximately 2 to 3 minutes). Drain, squeeze dry with your hands, and chop. You should have between 1 and 1½ cups of chopped spinach.

Cook the noodles in boiling, salted water until almost tender. Drain and set aside.

Melt the butter in a large (3- or 4-quart) saucepan. Add the scallions, garlic, and prosciutto or ham. Sauté until the scallions are soft. Lower the heat and stir in the flour. Cook, stirring, until well blended. Add the cream and continue to cook, stirring, until the sauce thickens and comes to a boil. Remove the sauce from the heat and stir in the noodles and spinach. Add salt to taste. Serve as is or spoon into a buttered shallow 2-quart casserole (8 by 11 inches). Sprinkle the top with cheese. Bake at 400°F for approximately 15 minutes or until the cheese browns and the sauce bubbles.

Summer Squash

Summer, zucchini, and scallop (Patty Pan) are all types of summer squash. They are quick-cooking, don't need to be peeled, may be steamed, blanched, or — my preference — sautéed. They also make good containers for stuffing after being parboiled for 5 to 10 minutes. Small scallop squash are particularly attractive stuffed for individual servings.

Zucchini, especially, lends itself to vegetable combinations. I often dice it and stir-fry it with fresh corn kernels and a little tomato. All the squashes combine nicely with dishes containing tomato. Summer (straightneck or crookneck) has a lovely, delicate flavor that I try not to overpower with herbs or combine with strong-flavored vegetables. I slice it thinly and sauté it in a little butter. It takes only 3 to 4 minutes to be cooked but not mushy. When I want to be fancy, I cut the summer squash into sticks (logs), add some slices of red pepper, and sauté them together in butter or oil. It's a beautiful color and taste combination that takes only about 4 minutes to cook.

Also, I grate either zucchini or summer squash (or both) on the large hole of my grater and sauté the squash in butter or oil, adding a clove of peeled garlic for flavor. Since a great deal of liquid cooks out, I remove the squash from the pan with a slotted spoon, leaving the liquid behind. If you wish to remove this liquid before cooking, place the grated squash in a colander, sprinkle lightly with salt, and let drain for 30 minutes. Squeeze the squash as dry as possible with your hands before cooking. It takes only about 3 minutes to cook the squash.

LOCAL SEASON: Mid-June to late September or frost

🌿 Summer Squash Casserole

Preheat the oven to 350°F. Butter a 1½-quart casserole.

1½ pounds summer squash
  (3 medium)
2 tablespoons butter or
  margarine
⅔ cup chopped onion
⅔ cup peeled, seeded, chopped
  uncooked tomato

½ cup sour cream
¼ cup bread crumbs
1 tablespoon grated Parmesan
  cheese
Salt and pepper to taste

Cut the squash into ¼-inch slices and cook in boiling, salted water or steam until almost tender. Drain it well and chop slightly.

Melt the butter in a small frying pan and add the onion. Sauté the onion until soft, then remove from the heat. Combine the squash and onion with the tomato, sour cream, bread crumbs, and salt and pepper. Spoon the mixture into the prepared casserole. Sprinkle the Parmesan cheese over the top. Bake at 350°F for 20 to 30 minutes or until the cheese melts and the squash is bubbly.

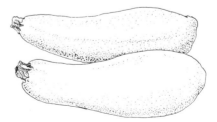

🌿 Stuffed Zucchini

SERVES 8

This recipe is best made with small zucchini, but when you don't have small ones, use medium to large squash and cut them in half crosswise and lengthwise after they have been parboiled. You need eight shells (halves) to stuff for individual servings.

Preheat the oven to 375°F. Grease a shallow 9-inch-square baking dish.

 4 small (2 medium) zucchini
¼ cup butter or margarine
⅔ cup chopped onion
⅓ cup chopped green pepper
 1 cup coarsely chopped
   mushrooms
½ cup bread crumbs
½ cup cottage cheese

¼ cup grated Parmesan or
   Romano cheese
½ teaspoon salt
1 to 2 tablespoons finely
   chopped dill (optional)
⅓ cup shredded Swiss or
   cheddar cheese

Parboil the whole zucchini in boiling, salted water for 5 to 10 minutes or until partially cooked. Drain and run under cold water until cool enough to handle. Cut the squash in half lengthwise so that you have eight pieces. Scoop out the pulp and seeds, then squeeze them partially dry, chop, and set aside. Place the zucchini shells in the prepared baking dish and make the stuffing.

Melt the butter in a large frying pan. Add the onion and pepper and sauté for 2 to 3 minutes. Add the reserved pulp and mushrooms. Continue to cook until the mushrooms soften. Remove from the heat and stir in the crumbs, cottage cheese, grated cheese, salt, and dill. Fill the zucchini shells and top with shredded cheese. Bake at 375°F for 25 to 30 minutes.

Winter Squash and Pumpkin

I group squash and pumpkin together because, when cooked and mashed, they are interchangeable in most recipes.

Winter Squash

The best known of the winter squashes are turban (the first to appear in late August), butternut, buttercup, Des Moines (acorn), and Hubbard. Vegetable spaghetti squash, while excellent, is not cooked and served in the same manner, although it is considered a winter squash.

Spaghetti squash has become so popular that it can no longer be considered a novelty. I cook it two ways. The whole unpeeled squash can be boiled in a large pot of water for about 30 minutes or until done. After draining, when it is cool enough to handle, cut it in half, remove the seeds, and scrape out the flesh with a fork, breaking it up into spaghetti-like strands. This is fine if you need a large amount of spaghetti squash. However, I often feed just two or three, so I cut the raw squash in half lengthwise, remove the seeds from one half (saving the other half for another dinner), and cook it in the oven like acorn squash. I put ½ inch of water in a shallow baking dish, place the squash, cut side down, in the water, and bake at 350°F for about 45 minutes. When the squash is done, I let it drain a few minutes, cut side down, in my colander, and then scrape out the squash strands. I serve spaghetti squash with butter, salt, and pepper. It is also good with grated cheese or tomato sauce.

Des Moines squash is usually baked in halves and offered as individual servings (recipe, page 178). I sometimes cut it crosswise into scalloped rings about ½ inch thick, removing the seeds but leaving the peel on. I steam the rings until tender. When I serve dinner plates (not family-style), I place a cooked ring on the plate and fill it with a green vegetable (peas, ½-inch pieces green beans, or chopped broccoli). When I want to serve the rings on a platter, I steam them until not quite done, then glaze them with brown sugar and butter in a large frying pan.

Buttercup squash, if not too large, may be baked like acorn. It is a lovely orange color, a darker and drier squash than acorn. Large squash may be used like butternut or Hubbard, which I generally steam or blanch in peeled chunks. Leaving the peel on changes the flavor. Steaming is the best method; it takes about 20 minutes to steam 2-inch chunks. Blanching takes less time — only about 10 minutes.

When you prepare squash or pumpkin to use in pies or other baked goods, it is important to drain it well. I don't use any salt when cooking the squash, preferring to add that with the other ingredients. I whip the cooked squash with my electric mixer to get the texture I want.

Winter squash may be peeled and grated and served raw in salads or grated and sautéed with butter or oil.

Pumpkin

Choose a sugar or New England pie pumpkin for cooking. These small, dark-orange pumpkins weigh 3 to 5 pounds. You can plan on at least ¾ cup of cooked, mashed pumpkin per pound. The larger field pumpkins grown for Halloween are stringy and not flavorful when cooked.

My young and enthusiastic editor, Genoa Shepley, told me that the problem of peeling a pumpkin intimidates her so much that she has never cooked it. That's a shame, since pumpkin is delicious. Peeling a pumpkin is really simple. You can always cut it into chunks with your trusty chef's knife and peel each chunk individually. Or place the pumpkin on a cutting board, cut off the bottom if it won't sit flat, and peel down the sides with a knife, turning the pumpkin slightly after each peeling stroke (you can peel fresh pineapple the same way). You can also steam pumpkin chunks with the skin still on and scrape the pumpkin from the skin when it's done, but I think it changes the pumpkin flavor. When the pumpkin is peeled, cut it into chunks, remove the seeds, and cook. Pumpkin and squash chunks take the same amount of time to cook.

Large pumpkins, while not good for cooking if heated, are excellent as soup tureens or serving containers for vegetables. Choose the size pumpkin you need, with no spots. Wash it and cut off the top, 1½ to 2 inches down for a tureen, 3 to 4 inches down for a container. You don't have to cut off as large a top because you use a ladle for a soup tureen. The top opening has to be larger in a vegetable container for ease in dishing out with a spoon. Save the top, cleaning off the inside of it. Clean out the pumpkin thoroughly, but take care not to make a hole in the bottom — it will leak! Cover the cleaned pumpkin with the top and bake it at 350°F for approximately 30 minutes or until heated through. Remove from the oven, drain any liquid, and fill with soup or vegetables. It's great for buffet tables as it keeps food hot while looking good.

Don't store whole squash or pumpkin in the refrigerator. Keep them in a dry area at room temperature.

LOCAL SEASON: Spaghetti — available late July to early October

Turban — harvested mid-August, available through Thanksgiving

Butternut — harvested late August, available through March

Buttercup — harvested late August, available into January

Des Moines — harvested late August, available through Thanksgiving

Hubbard — harvested early September but not sold until mid-October after it has cured (dried), available through March

Pumpkins — available early September to November

🌿 Very Easy Grated Winter Squash

SERVES 4 TO 6

This dish takes almost no time to cook, and the grating may be done early in the day. Any winter squash — butternut, turban, Hubbard, or buttercup — is excellent for this recipe. If you buy peeled butternut squash, use 1½ to 2 pounds.

6 to 7 cups peeled, grated squash
2 to 3 tablespoons butter or margarine
Salt and pepper to taste

1 to 2 tablespoons brown sugar (optional)
Dash cinnamon (optional)

Remove the seeds and peel from 2 to 2½ pounds of squash. Cut the raw squash into chunks and grate on the large holes of a grater. Melt the butter in a large frying pan. Add the squash and sauté, stirring for 4 to 5 minutes or until the squash is heated through. Add 1 tablespoon of water if the squash seems to be dry or sticks to the pan. Add salt and pepper and, for sweet squash, the sugar and cinnamon.

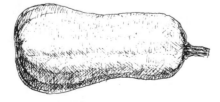

🍂 Winter Squash or Pumpkin Casserole

This casserole is equally good made with winter squash, such as butternut or Hubbard, or sugar pumpkin. At our house, it is traditional at Thanksgiving, but I also serve it to company since it can be prepared the day before and cooked just before serving.

Preheat the oven to 350°F.

$2^{1}/_{2}$ to 3 pounds peeled squash
    or pumpkin
  2 tablespoons butter or
    margarine
  $^{1}/_{8}$ teaspoon cinnamon

$1^{1}/_{2}$ tablespoons brown sugar
  $^{1}/_{2}$ cup brown sugar
  $^{1}/_{3}$ cup chopped nuts

Cut the squash or pumpkin into chunks and cook in boiling, salted water or steam until tender. Drain thoroughly in a colander. Return the hot squash to the pan and add the butter, cinnamon, and $1^{1}/_{2}$ tablespoons of brown sugar. Whip together with an electric mixer or mash until smooth. Place the mixture in a $1^{1}/_{2}$- to 2-quart casserole. Sprinkle the top with $^{1}/_{2}$ cup of brown sugar and the chopped nuts. Bake at 350°F for 25 to 30 minutes.

NOTE: The casserole may be made ahead of time and refrigerated without the brown sugar and nuts. These should be added just before baking. If the casserole has been refrigerated, adjust the baking time.

🌺 Baked Des Moines (Acorn) Squash

To bake Des Moines squash without stuffing, cut the squash in half from stem to blossom end. Remove the seeds and place the halves, cut side down, in a shallow baking dish. Fill the dish with hot water to a depth of ½ to ¾ inch. Bake at 350°F for 30 minutes, then turn the squash over. Place some butter (a teaspoon or so) in each half, sprinkle the insides with salt and pepper, and continue to bake, uncovered, until the squash is tender — 10 to 20 minutes, depending on its size. Brush butter over the sides of the squash two to three times during this period. If you prefer sweet squash, eliminate the salt and pepper and use brown sugar with butter in the squash.

🌺 Apple-Stuffed Des Moines (Acorn) Squash

Preheat the oven to 350°F.

3 small (1 pound each) Des Moines squash
¼ cup butter, melted
Dash cinnamon
3 apples, peeled and chopped into small pieces

1 tablespoon lemon juice
½ cup brown sugar
½ cup chopped walnuts (optional)

Cut 3 small or 2 medium squash in half from stem to blossom end. Remove the seeds. Place, cut side down, in a shallow baking dish. fill the dish with hot water to a depth of ½ to ¾ inch. Bake at 350°F for 30 minutes. Turn the squash over. Brush the insides and cut areas with some of the melted butter. Sprinkle with cinnamon. Set aside.

Combine the apples (you should have about 3 cups of pieces), lemon juice, remaining butter, brown sugar, and walnuts in a mixing bowl. Fill the squash halves with the apple mixture. Cover the entire baking dish with foil. Continue to bake for approximately 30 minutes longer or until both the apples and squash are tender.

Tomatoes

Everyone who gardens has their favorite tomato variety. I dearly love Beefsteak tomatoes, but I must admit my father, Ray Culler's, Supersonics are pretty tasty. Jet Star is the tomato most commonly grown in Massachusetts, commercially and in home gardens, but other varieties, both old standbys and newly developed ones, are also popular.

I really think that the best way to eat tomatoes is at room temperature (chilled tomatoes, like most fruit, have less flavor) with a little salt and pepper. Of course, tomato sandwiches with mayonnaise are also one of my weaknesses. My father, who has always had a large garden (and a sweet tooth), puts sugar on his sliced tomatoes. I suppose, considering that tomatoes are truly a fruit, this is not outrageous.

During the summer, we have sliced tomatoes at most meals. I don't generally peel them when I serve them sliced (not even for company), but in casseroles or other cooked dishes, peeling is important. Fortunately, it is very simple. Bring a pot of water to a boil and dip the tomato into the boiling water for 5 to 10 seconds. It's best to dip tomatoes one at a time in order to avoid cooking them, which makes them mushy. Also core tomatoes *after* dipping them in the water. The skin peels off easily. To seed, cut the tomato in half across the middle (not stem to blossom end) and gently squeeze each half until the seeds fall out, or remove the seeds with your fingers or a small spoon.

Cherry tomatoes are usually reserved for salads and are seldom served hot, which is too bad. If you sauté them in butter or margarine for only a minute or two (just until they are heated through; they explode if cooked too long), they are scrumptious. Sprinkle them with chopped fresh basil (or any other herb) and they are even better.

LOCAL SEASON: Tomatoes — mid-July to late September or frost
                Cherry tomatoes — late July to late September or frost

🌿 *Tomato Casserole*

This is a favorite recipe because it can be put together early in the day and baked just before serving.

Preheat the oven to 350°F. Butter a deep 1½-quart casserole.

*1½ to 2 pounds ripe tomatoes
  (4 or 5 medium)*
*4 tablespoons butter or
  margarine*
*⅔ cup chopped green
  pepper*

½ cup chopped onion
⅔ cup bread crumbs
½ teaspoon salt
⅛ teaspoon pepper

Peel and slice the tomatoes ⅓ to ½ inch thick.

Melt the butter in a small frying pan. Add the pepper and onion and sauté over medium heat until soft but not brown. Remove from the heat and stir in the crumbs, salt, and pepper.

Place the tomato slices and crumb mixture in the prepared casserole in three or four layers, starting with the tomatoes and ending with the crumbs. Bake, uncovered, at 350°F for 35 to 45 minutes or until the tomatoes are soft and the crumbs brown.

🌿 Tomatoes Stuffed with Zucchini

SERVES 6

When you pick out tomatoes for this recipe, select ones with flat bottoms, so that they will sit straight when you serve them.

Preheat the oven to 350°F.

6 small tomatoes (2 to 2½ inches in diameter)

3 tablespoons butter or margarine

½ cup chopped onion

1 teaspoon minced garlic

¾ cup bread crumbs

2½ cups coarsely shredded zucchini

½ teaspoon salt

⅛ teaspoon pepper

2 tablespoons grated Parmesan cheese

Remove the tops from the tomatoes and carefully scoop out the pulp. Discard the seeds but chop the remaining pulp. Set aside. Sprinkle the insides of the tomato shells with salt and turn upside down to drain for 15 minutes. While the tomatoes drain, make the stuffing.

Melt the butter in a medium frying pan. Add the onion and garlic and sauté over medium heat until soft. Stir in the bread crumbs, zucchini, reserved tomato pulp, salt, pepper, and 1 tablespoon of the cheese. Cook, stirring, until heated through but not cooked. Remove from the heat. Dry the insides of the tomato shells with paper towels. Fill the shells with stuffing and sprinkle the tops with the remaining tablespoon of cheese. Place in a shallow baking pan. Bake at 350°F for 15 to 20 minutes or until the tomatoes are soft. Do not overcook.

Turnips

I remember that when I was a child, turnips (especially rutabagas) had a strong, unpleasant taste. If that is your memory, too, try turnips now. Over the years, new varieties have been developed that have a delicious, mild flavor totally unlike the turnips of my childhood.

Purple-top turnips may be peeled and blanched until soft in boiling, salted water. Whole 2-inch turnips take about 30 minutes to cook, while ½-inch cubes take about 15. The turnips may then be drained and served as is with butter or sauce, or mashed with butter. However, I prefer to sauté turnips rather than boil them. Peel and slice the turnips thinly. Sauté the slices in butter or oil (or a combination) in a large frying pan for 5 to 10 minutes. Add salt and pepper. If the slices don't soften quickly enough, cover the pan and let them steam for a minute or two. The sautéed slices are lovely. I also serve both purple-top turnips and rutabagas raw on vegetable and dip trays. They may be cut into slices or sticks (like carrots). People don't recognize the flavor, but they like it.

Rutabagas are one of my all-time favorites. I love the flavor of these big yellow turnips. When I peel one prior to cooking, I'm likely to eat half of it raw. I blanch the peeled rutabaga pieces in boiling, salted water. Depending on the size of the peeled pieces, they take 25 to 35 minutes to cook. I drain them well and whip them with my electric mixer, adding some butter or margarine. If the dish is to be served for a holiday dinner (it's traditionally one of our many vegetables at Thanksgiving), I add a tablespoon of brown sugar and a dash of cinnamon.

LOCAL SEASON: Purple tops — mid-September to Thanksgiving
                 Rutabagas — late August to November

Better Butter

2 butter   ——— room temperature
1 C olive oil
1 C Canola

blend or food process til
smooth. Pour into containers

CRANBERRY - APPLE CRISP

Mix together

- 1½ cups whole cranberries
- 6 cups peeled apples in ½" pieces
- 3/4 cup sugar
- 1/4 teaspoon cinnamon

Pour mixture into buttered 9" square pan.

With fork or fingers, mix the following together to make streusel topping

- 1/2 cup flour
- 1/2 cup quick cooking oatmeal
- 5 tablespoons butter or margarine (softened)
- 1/3 cup dark brown sugar (packed)
- 1/2 teaspoon cinnamon
  dash cloves

Spoon topping over cranberry mixture.
Bake 50 to 55 minutes at 350° until fruit in center of dish is soft.

Serve warm with ice cream.

CREAM OF MUSHROOM SOUP

In large pan, saute for 2 to 3 minutes
    1 pound mushrooms, trimmed and cut into
    large slices (4-4 1/2 cups), in
    4 tablespoons butter
Add 3 cups chicken broth
    2/3 cup chopped celery
    1/3 cup chopped onion
Simmer 20-30 minutes until vegetables are very
tender. Puree and set aside.
Make a cream sauce as follows:
Melt over low heat
    3 tablespoons butter
Stir in
    3 tablespoons flour
Cook 1 to 2 minutes - remove from heat.
Add slowly, stirring constantly
    1 1/3 cups milk
Return to heat.
Cook and stir until sauce comes to a boil.
Cook 1 minute longer, stirring - remove from
 heat

Stir puree into cream sauce
Salt and pepper to taste
Stir in 2 tablespoons dry white wine, if desired.

Return to low heat - heat gently - do not boil.
Just before serving, top with a heaping
tablespoon of unsweetened whipped cream.

Serves 6.

Growing Since 1884

Wilson Farms, Inc.

10 Pleasant Street, Lexington, MA 02421 • (781) 862-3900

<u>EASY BUTTERNUT SQUASH OR PUMPKIN CASSEROLE</u>

Cook 2 1/2 to 3 pounds of peeled pumpkin or squash chunks
in boiling, salted water (or steam) until tender.
Drain thoroughly.

Whip together with electric mixer

  Squash
  1/4 Cup butter or margarine
  1/8 teaspoon cinnamon
  1/2 tablespoons dark brown sugar

Place squash mixture in 1 1/2 quart casserole

Sprinkle top with

  1/2 Cup dark brown sugar
  1/3 Cup chopped walnuts or pecans

Bake at 350° 20-30 minutes
Serves 8

This may be made ahead of time and refrigerated
without topping. Add topping just before baking.
If casserole is cold, adjust baking time.

Growing Since 1884

🌺 *Rutabaga Casserole*

SERVES 6

This slightly sweet, custardy casserole appeals even to those people who don't care for the flavor of yellow turnip.

Preheat the oven to 350°F. Butter a deep 1-quart casserole.

2 cups peeled, cooked, mashed rutabaga
2 eggs, well beaten
1 cup milk or light cream, scalded
2 tablespoons butter or margarine

2 tablespoons brown sugar
⅛ teaspoon nutmeg
Salt to taste

Peel and dice the rutabaga. Blanch in boiling, salted water for 25 to 30 minutes. Purée or mash very well.

Beat the eggs in a mixing bowl and beat in the rutabaga and the remaining ingredients. Spoon into the prepared casserole. Place the casserole in a shallow pan. Pour very hot water into the pan to a depth of 1 inch (cook like a custard). Bake at 350°F for approximately 1 hour or until set. Let rest 10 minutes before serving.

6

*Main
Courses*

*O*ur son, Scott, was convinced that I was never going to get around to writing a main-course chapter. When he was home from college, I was testing desserts and salads. Now, he likes desserts and salads, but he is also a practical, down-to-earth, hungry young man who feels the need for something more filling. I'm sure he'll be relieved to see this chapter.

There is no rhyme or reason for my choice of main-course recipes. Most are dishes that my family is particularly fond of or that I like to serve at parties. We sell hamburger from our dairy farm in Maine at our farm stand, but that is the only red meat we carry. We sell poultry of all types — turkeys, geese, ducks, and Rock Cornish hens year round — but, naturally, sales are greater at the holidays. Fresh chicken is available at all times, and I have included many chicken recipes in this chapter. I use more chicken than any other meat (we not only like it, but it is available only a few steps from my door!) so I try new recipes for chicken frequently.

❧ Roasting Poultry

There are so many different methods of cooking poultry that I hesitate to recommend a particular one. However, I do offer some suggestions for roasting poultry.

Chicken

When you buy chicken, it is important to select the proper type for the way you plan to cook it. Although there is very little distinction between broilers and fryers, I select a smaller chicken for broiling than for frying. Roasting chickens may be cooked with dry heat in the oven, but fowl, also called stewing chickens or hens, need moist heat. I use fowl when a recipe calls for cut-up chicken or when I want to make chicken broth. Fowl take longer to cook, but their flavor is superior for that purpose. Incidentally, Don Wilson, one of the farm owners, told me that, technically, chickens become fowl as soon as they start laying eggs, at about 20 weeks.

Roast chicken is delicious stuffed or unstuffed. I roast a stuffed 5- to 6-pound chicken at 375°F for about 2 hours. For an unstuffed chicken, 1½ hours is usually enough time. Place the chicken on a rack in a shallow pan, breast side down. Halfway through the roasting time, turn the chicken breast side up and complete the cooking to ensure that the breast meat remains moist. I don't baste the chicken, but I sometimes glaze it for a special treat.

Broiler-fryer chickens (9 to 10 weeks)   2½ to 3½ pounds
Roasting chickens (16 to 18 weeks)   4 to 6 pounds
Fowl, stewing chickens (over 1 year)   5 to 6 pounds

BONING CHICKEN BREASTS

Some people are confused over the distinction between single chicken breasts and whole chicken breasts. Each live chicken has one whole breast with two sides. Many stores sell whole breasts as a unit. We sell packages containing four pieces of single breasts, which are really two whole breasts (both sides) that have been split in half to give single serving pieces. My recipes are for these pieces, which I refer to as breasts.

Boning chicken breasts is no big deal. You can buy them already boned, but it is quite simple to bone them yourself. Remove the skin, if you want skinless chicken, before boning by simply pulling it off. It is easiest to bone chicken breasts when you have a boning knife, but a sharp, good-sized paring knife will work. Place the breast, bone down, on a cutting board. Cut between the flesh and bone at the narrow end. Continue to cut and scrape the chicken away from the bone, trying not to tear the flesh. Working gradually, pull the chicken flesh back with your fingers as you cut so you can see where you are cutting. When the chicken is separated from the bone, remove the white tendon by pulling it and scraping the chicken from it.

Don't panic when you leave more meat on the bones than you'd hoped. I do it all the time. Just cook up the bones in some water (as you would a fowl to make Chicken Broth). Add some sliced onion, celery, bay leaf, salt, and pepper to the water, and let it all simmer for an hour or so. You'll soon have broth. Pull the meat off the bones and make chicken soup. No waste, and your family will enjoy your homemade chicken soup. Add rice or noodles and the chicken you've removed from the bones to the boiling broth, season, and serve.

Turkey

I plan on 15 minutes per pound at 350°F for fresh turkeys. I also allow an extra hour just in case the turkey doesn't get done in that length of time. On the other hand, overcooking a turkey dries it out. A turkey should rest for 30 minutes after being removed from the oven before carving, so the extra time provides the rest period as well as a cushion in case the turkey has to roast longer. I grease the turkey with a little soft butter before roasting and place it on a rack in a large roasting pan. Unless I'm cooking an enormous turkey that I can't lift, I cook the turkey breast side down for a little more than half the roasting period, then turn it breast side up. If the breast skin appears to be browning too much toward the end of the cooking time, I tent it loosely with foil. A meat thermometer should read 180°F to 185°F when the turkey is done.

It is best to thaw frozen turkey in the refrigerator, which takes 2 to 3 days.

Goose

Since I began to cook geese much later than other forms of poultry, I'm still a relative novice. I have found that fresh geese always take less time to cook than I expect. A meat thermometer is a great help. A 12-pound goose roasts in about 3 hours (15 minutes per pound), but it should be checked after 2½ hours. I roast the goose breast side up on a rack in a shallow pan at 325°F. I find it necessary to drain the fat from the pan once or twice during the cooking period. Fruit stuffing is particularly good with goose.

Duck

I would rather have roast duck than almost any other meat. I am partial to the dark meat of poultry, so, of course, duck and goose are my main choices. I cut my ducks in half before roasting, but they may also be cut in quarters or cooked whole. I don't stuff duck, preferring to serve it with wild rice, mushrooms, and a green salad. Roast a duck at 325°F on a rack in a shallow pan. Prick the skin with a fork only over the very fatty areas, not the entire bird. A 5-pound duck takes about 1½ to 2 hours to cook. When I glaze a duck, I roast it for about 1½ hours, then apply the glaze often during the remainder of the cooking time.

Rock Cornish Hens

These should be baked at 375°F for about 1 hour, breast side down for the first half-hour. Most stuffings freeze well, so when you make stuffing for a turkey or chicken and have a little left over, freeze it for future use in one of these tiny, single-serving birds. They should be brushed with melted butter several times while they bake. They are also good lightly glazed.

❧ Stuffing for Poultry

This recipe is my version of my mother-in-law, Edith Wilson's, turkey stuffing. She always used half Ritz cracker crumbs, which she made by rolling the crackers with her rolling pin. Of course, life is simpler now — I use my food processor to make crumbs.

3/4 cup butter or margarine
2 cups finely chopped celery
1 1/2 cups finely chopped onion
5 cups Ritz cracker crumbs
5 cups dry bread crumbs

2 to 3 tablespoons poultry seasoning
2 teaspoons salt (or to taste)
1/4 teaspoon ground pepper
2 to 2 1/2 cups Chicken Broth (recipe, page 40)

Melt the butter in a large frying pan. Add the celery and onion and sauté until soft. Set aside.

Combine the cracker crumbs, bread crumbs, poultry seasoning, salt, and pepper in a large mixing bowl. Stir in the onion, celery, and butter from the frying pan. Add enough broth to moisten thoroughly.

NOTE: You may use all bread crumbs, but the Ritz crackers add a nice flavor. I sometimes add 1 1/2 cups of chopped nuts or 1 1/2 pounds of sliced and sautéed mushrooms to my stuffing.

❦ Cornbread and Sausage Stuffing

MAKES ENOUGH FOR A 14-POUND TURKEY

My mother, Nan Culler, a Southerner, always made cornbread stuffing and giblet gravy for our Thanksgiving turkey. She sometimes added sausage and chestnuts. I, too, add sausage, but, as a mushroom lover, I substitute mushrooms for the chestnuts.

Preheat the oven to 425°F. Grease an 8-inch-square pan.

CORNBREAD

1 cup yellow cornmeal	1/2 teaspoon salt
1 cup flour	1 cup milk
4 teaspoons baking powder	1 egg
2 teaspoons poultry seasoning	1/3 cup oil

Combine the cornmeal, flour, baking powder, poultry seasoning, and salt in a mixing bowl. Beat in the milk, egg, and oil with an electric mixer or spoon until smooth. Pour into the prepared pan and bake at 425°F for approximately 20 minutes or until done. Cool the cornbread before proceeding with the stuffing.

STUFFING

6 tablespoons butter or margarine	1/2 pound sausage meat, cooked and drained
1 cup chopped onion	1 cup Chicken Broth (recipe, page 40)
3/4 cup chopped celery	Salt and pepper to taste
2 cups sliced mushrooms	

Crumble the cooled cornbread into small pieces and place them in a large mixing bowl. Set aside.

Melt the butter in a large frying pan over medium heat and add the onion, celery, and mushrooms. Sauté the vegetables until they soften and add them to the cornbread crumbs. Add the cooked sausage meat and mix. Stir in the broth and season to taste.

🌺 Apple Stuffing

Several years ago, because of the great demand for fresh geese at
Christmas, we started to raise them. Until then, I had never
cooked a goose. When Jan Fox, one of our employees, told me she
had an apple stuffing recipe for goose, I decided to give it a try.
Goose has become a favorite at our house. The meat is all dark
and not at all greasy. This recipe is good for any poultry. However,
when you use it for chicken or duck, you have to adjust the
amounts of the ingredients.

2/3 cup butter or margarine	3 cups 1/4- to 1/2-inch-diced apples
3/4 cup chopped onion	1/4 cup finely chopped parsley
3/4 cup chopped celery	1 1/2 teaspoons salt (or to taste)
1 clove garlic, peeled and minced	1/8 teaspoon pepper
6 cups fresh bread crumbs	1 cup raisins

Melt the butter in a large frying pan over medium heat. Add the
onion, celery, and garlic and sauté until soft but not brown.

Place the bread crumbs in a large mixing bowl. Add the butter and
vegetables and mix thoroughly. Stir in the apples, parsley, salt, pepper, and raisins. Stuff the bird loosely without packing. The stuffing, which is quite dry, absorbs juices from the apples and the
goose as they cook.

NOTE: Use a blender or food processor to make fresh bread
crumbs. Be careful not to make the crumbs too fine. Small pieces
of bread with some texture work best. You can also make crumbs
by hand — simply break the fresh bread into very small pieces
with your fingers.

❧ Cranberry-Raisin-Nut Stuffing

MAKES ENOUGH FOR A 16- TO 18-POUND TURKEY

2 cups coarsely chopped
  cranberries
1/2 cup sugar
1/2 cup butter or margarine
3/4 cup chopped onion
1 cup chopped celery
4 cups dry bread crumbs

1 teaspoon poultry seasoning
1/2 teaspoon salt
3/4 cup chopped walnuts
1 cup raisins (plumped, if
  desired)
1 cup Chicken Broth (recipe,
  page 40)

Stir the chopped cranberries and sugar together and set aside.

Melt the butter in a frying pan over medium heat. Add the onion
and celery and sauté until soft. Remove from the heat.

Place the bread crumbs, poultry seasoning, salt, walnuts, raisins,
and broth in a large mixing bowl. Stir them together and then stir
in the onion, celery, and butter mixture. Stir in the cranberries and
sugar. Stuff the turkey loosely.

NOTE: To plump raisins, pour enough boiling water over them to
just cover. Let them sit for about 5 minutes, drain thoroughly and
add.

🌿 Poultry Glazes

Either of these glazes may be used on any poultry, but I usually reserve them for duck.

Orange Glaze

MAKES GLAZE FOR TWO DUCKS

½ cup undiluted frozen orange
   juice concentrate
⅓ cup orange marmalade
1 tablespoon Worcestershire
   sauce

¼ teaspoon dry mustard
8 thin slices orange

Place all the ingredients, except the orange slices, in a small saucepan. Simmer, uncovered, over low heat for 4 to 5 minutes. Using a brush, glaze the duck often during the final 15 to 30 minutes of roasting. Five minutes before the cooking is completed, place the thin slices of unpeeled orange on the duck, brush with the glaze, and cook with the duck until the orange softens.

NOTE: Regular orange juice may be used, but the undiluted frozen is more satisfactory.

Peach Glaze

MAKES GLAZE FOR 1 DUCK

½ cup orange juice
¼ cup peach brandy
1 tablespoon cornstarch

1 to 2 whole cloves
1 teaspoon brown sugar
2 to 3 peaches

Mix the orange juice, brandy, cornstarch, cloves, and brown sugar in a small saucepan, stirring until the cornstarch dissolves. Cook over medium-low heat until the glaze becomes less cloudy.

Peel the peaches and cut them into quarters and add to the glaze. Poach until they soften (3 to 5 minutes). Remove the peach quarters and set aside.

Using a brush, glaze the duck often during the final 15 to 30 minutes of roasting. Reheat the peach quarters and serve with the duck.

Wild Rice

SERVES 4 TO 6

 1 cup uncooked wild rice
 3½ cups Chicken Broth (recipe,
       page 40)
 4 tablespoons butter or
       margarine
 ½ cup sliced scallions
 2 cups sliced mushrooms
       Salt and pepper to taste

Wash the rice. Place it in a 3-quart saucepan with the broth. Cover and bring to a boil. Uncover and boil for 5 minutes. Reduce the heat, cover, and simmer until the liquid is almost absorbed (45 to 55 minutes).

While the rice is cooking, melt the butter in a frying pan, add the scallions and mushrooms, and sauté until they soften. Set aside.

When the rice liquid is almost absorbed, stir in the scallions, mushrooms, and any liquid in the pan. Continue to cook the rice, uncovered, until it is done and the liquid absorbed (15 to 20 minutes). Stir often. Season to taste.

NOTE: When I have leftover glaze, I stir it into the rice, which is especially nice with Orange Glaze (recipe, page 194).

❧ Turkey Tetrazzini

SERVES 6

Leftover Thanksgiving turkey, dressed up in this recipe, makes an excellent dish for a buffet table.

Preheat the oven to 400°F. Butter a shallow 2-quart casserole.

1 cup milk	$^1/_4$ cup sherry
1 cup Chicken Broth (recipe, page 40)	$^3/_4$ cup heavy cream
$^1/_2$ cup butter or margarine	$^1/_2$ pound uncooked thin spaghetti
$^1/_2$ cup flour	2 cups sliced mushrooms
$^1/_2$ teaspoon salt (or to taste)	3 cups diced, cooked turkey
$^1/_4$ teaspoon pepper	$^1/_4$ cup milk, if necessary
Pinch nutmeg	$^1/_3$ cup grated Parmesan cheese

Heat the 1 cup of milk and the broth together. Meanwhile, melt 6 tablespoons of the butter in a 3-quart saucepan. Stir the flour into the butter. Cook, stirring, until well blended. Stir in the hot milk and broth. Cook until smooth and thick. Remove from the heat and stir in the salt, pepper, nutmeg, sherry, and cream.

Cook and drain the spaghetti.

Sauté the mushrooms until soft in the remaining 2 tablespoons of butter. Combine the turkey, mushrooms, sauce, and spaghetti. Mix well. If the mixture appears to be too thick, stir in the $^1/_4$ cup milk. Turn into the prepared casserole. Top with the cheese. Bake at 400°F for approximately 20 minutes or until the cheese melts and the sauce is bubbly.

NOTE: Cooked chicken may be substituted for turkey.

❧Chicken Cacciatore

SERVES 4 TO 6

This good dish tastes even better when prepared in advance and reheated. I use a large electric frying pan, but it may be made in a large soup pot. It is one of our daughter Lesley's favorite dishes.

1/3 cup oil

8 to 12 pieces chicken (depending on size — approximately 3½ to 4 pounds)

6 cups peeled, chopped tomatoes (seeded, if desired — 3½ to 4 pounds)

2 large green peppers, sliced (¾ pound total)

1 large yellow onion, sliced (½ pound)

1 pound mushrooms, sliced

1 clove garlic, minced

¼ teaspoon dried oregano (1 to 2 teaspoons fresh)

2 teaspoons chopped fresh basil

1 teaspoon salt

⅛ teaspoon pepper

Grated Parmesan cheese

Spaghetti or rice (optional)

Heat the oil in a very large, deep frying pan. Add the chicken and cook over medium-high heat, uncovered, turning once, for about 10 minutes or until lightly brown. Lower the heat slightly and cover the pan. Continue to cook for 10 minutes longer. Drain the fat and accumulated juices from the pan. Add the tomatoes, peppers, onion, mushrooms, garlic, oregano, basil, salt, and pepper. Cover the pan and let the vegetables cook down to make the sauce (5 to 10 minutes). Uncover and simmer for 25 to 30 minutes, turning the chicken occasionally, until the vegetables are done and the sauce has thickened slightly. Top with grated Parmesan cheese and serve over spaghetti or rice.

NOTE: Seeded tomatoes produce a less liquid sauce than unseeded, so when you plan to serve it over spaghetti or rice, do not discard the seeds. Legs and thighs should be separated since they take considerably longer to cook when together.

❧ Orange-Cranberry Chicken

SERVES 4 TO 6

8 to 9 pieces chicken (1 cut-up
    fryer with legs and thighs
    separated)
    Salt
  2 tablespoons butter or
    margarine
  ½ cup chopped onion

¾ cup orange juice
 1 tablespoon cornstarch
¼ cup orange liqueur
 2 cups whole cranberries
¼ cup dark brown sugar
¼ cup granulated sugar

Sprinkle the chicken pieces with salt. Melt the butter in a large frying pan, add the chicken, and brown over medium heat. Remove the chicken from the pan, add the onion, and sauté until soft but not brown. Lower the heat and stir in the orange juice and cornstarch. Continue stirring until the cornstarch is dissolved. Add the liqueur, cranberries, brown sugar, and granulated sugar. Simmer over low heat until the cranberries burst. Return the chicken pieces to the pan, cover, and simmer for approximately 45 minutes, turning the chicken and basting often until it is tender. Serve with the sauce.

NOTE: If you prefer, eliminate the liqueur and use 1 cup of orange juice.

❧Chicken Salad

SERVES ABOUT 6

Follow the recipe for Chicken Broth on page 40, to get the 6 cups of meat.

6 cups diced, cooked chicken (approximate)

1½ cups chopped celery

2 tablespoons finely chopped onion

1 tablespoon lemon juice

3 tablespoons salad oil

½ teaspoon salt

⅛ teaspoon pepper

1 cup mayonnaise

Mix the warm chicken with the celery, onion, lemon juice, oil, salt, and pepper. Stir until thoroughly mixed. Chill until it is almost time to serve, then stir in the mayonnaise and correct the seasoning.

NOTE: When you stir in the mayonnaise, add ½ cup of chopped nuts, chopped apple, drained canned pineapple, or some chopped parsley for variety.

❧ Boneless Chicken Breasts with Mushrooms

SERVES 4 TO 8, DEPENDING ON THE SIZE OF THE CHICKEN BREASTS

This is a nice dish to serve to guests. When I put it on a buffet table with other main course selections, I cut the boneless chicken breasts in half. The pieces are easier to manage, and I also find that given a selection of main courses, my friends like to try a little of everything, and a whole chicken breast is too much.

½ cup flour	½ cup thinly sliced scallions
1 teaspoon salt	1½ cups light cream
⅛ teaspoon pepper	1 cup Chicken Broth (recipe, page 40)
½ cup butter or margarine	⅓ cup sherry
8 to 10 chicken breasts, skinned and boned (see page 187)	
4 cups sliced mushrooms (about 1 pound)	

Mix the flour, salt, and pepper in a shallow dish or pan.

Melt the butter in a very large frying pan over medium heat.

Dredge the chicken pieces in the flour mixture and brown both sides lightly in the butter. Remove from the butter and set aside. Save the remaining flour mixture — you will need 1½ tablespoons of it. Add the mushrooms and scallions to the butter and sauté until they start to soften. Sprinkle with the 1½ tablespoons flour. Stir in the cream, broth, and sherry. Return the chicken to the pan and simmer, uncovered, for about 10 to 15 minutes or until the chicken is done and the sauce has thickened. Correct the seasoning.

NOTE: When I serve this dish to my family, I often use unboned legs and thighs, because we prefer dark meat. It is just as good as the breasts but takes a little longer to cook.

❧ Stir-Fried Chicken with Asparagus and Mushrooms

SERVES 3 TO 4

4 chicken breasts, skinned
   and boned (see page
   187)
2 tablespoons sherry
1 tablespoon soy sauce
2 tablespoons water
1 tablespoon cornstarch
2 teaspoons sugar
1 clove garlic, peeled and
   minced
1/4 to 1/2 teaspoon grated ginger
   root (1/4 teaspoon
   ground ginger)

1/4 teaspoon salt
4 tablespoons oil
1/2 cup thinly sliced scallions
2 cups 1/2-inch diagonally sliced
   pieces asparagus
2 cups 1/4-inch-sliced
   mushrooms

Cut the chicken breasts into 2-inch pieces. Mix the sherry, soy sauce, water, cornstarch, sugar, garlic, ginger root, and salt in a small bowl. Add the chicken and stir to coat. Marinate in the refrigerator for at least 1 hour. Just before serving, heat 3 tablespoons of the oil in a large frying pan over medium-high. Add the scallions, asparagus, and mushrooms. Stir-fry for 3 to 4 minutes or until the mushrooms and asparagus soften slightly. Remove the vegetables from the pan, add the remaining tablespoon of oil and the chicken. Stir-fry the chicken for 4 to 5 minutes or until almost done. Return the vegetables to the pan, add any remaining marinade, and continue to cook, stirring, for another 2 to 3 minutes or until the flavors are well blended. Serve immediately.

NOTE: Fresh shelled and deveined shrimp (3/4 to 1 pound) may be substituted for chicken. Stir-fry the shrimp for only 2 to 3 minutes or until it turns pink. The rest of the cooking times and ingredients are the same as for chicken.

❧ Boneless Chicken Breasts Stuffed with Spinach and Cheese

SERVES 8

There are two ways to cook these — both good. The stuffed rolls may be fried in a minimum of fat or baked in the oven and served with a tarragon or dill sauce. Whether you bake or fry the rolls, the chicken becomes firm as it cooks. Just make sure the chicken surrounds the stuffing and it will stay together. Read the entire recipe through before you start, because the first set of ingredients is only for the stuffing, not cooking. The recipe for the sauce, which is as good with fish as with chicken, is at the end. The herb you choose is a matter of personal taste.

2 pounds fresh spinach
   (1½ pounds trimmed)
8 large chicken breasts, skinned
   and boned (see page 187)
4 tablespoons butter or
   margarine
⅓ cup thinly sliced scallions

⅓ cup bread crumbs
1 cup coarsely grated Swiss
   cheese
½ teaspoon salt
   Pepper to taste

Wash and trim the spinach. Place it in a large pot with the water remaining on the leaves. Cook over medium-low heat only until the spinach wilts. Drain well, run cold water over the spinach to stop the cooking, and squeeze it as dry as possible with your hands. Chop the spinach. You need 1½ cups.

Flatten (pound) the chicken breasts into ¼-inch-thick cutlets with a mallet or rolling pin.

Melt the butter in a large frying pan over medium heat. Add the scallions and sauté until they soften. Add the spinach and cook, stirring, for 1 to 2 minutes. Remove from the heat and stir in the bread crumbs, cheese, salt, and pepper. Divide the stuffing mixture into eight parts. Place one portion on each flattened chicken breast and roll up or fold in the sides to enclose.

TO FRY

1 egg
1 tablespoon water
⅔ cup bread crumbs
⅓ teaspoon salt

⅛ teaspoon pepper
4 to 6 tablespoons oil or
   shortening

Beat the egg and water together in a shallow pan. Mix the bread-crumbs, salt, and pepper in another shallow pan. Roll each stuffed chicken breast in the egg and then in the crumbs to coat lightly. Fry in a minimum of fat (no more than ¼ inch), turning four times (one-quarter turn each time), until the rolls are completely brown on all sides — about 15 minutes. When fried, these are good with or without the sauce.

TO BAKE

Preheat the oven to 400°F.

Make the rolls as directed and place them in a shallow 9-by-13-inch baking dish, seam side down.

²⁄₃ cup Chicken Broth (recipe,
    page 40)
    Tarragon or Dill Sauce

Pour the broth into the bottom of the baking dish. Cover the pan tightly with foil. Bake at 400°F for about 30 minutes or until done. Top with the sauce.

Tarragon or Dill Sauce

Meg Stewart, one of my loyal taste-testers in the farm office, said it would be heavenly if she could have more sauce and some rice. The amount of sauce in the recipe is just enough to top the chicken breasts. If you serve it with rice, double the recipe.

2 tablespoons butter
1 tablespoon finely chopped
    shallots
2 tablespoons flour
1 cup Chicken Broth (recipe,
    page 40)

1 tablespoon finely chopped
    fresh tarragon or dill
    Salt (optional)

Melt the butter in a small saucepan. Stir in the shallots and cook for about 1 minute or until they soften. Stir in the flour and cook for 1 minute. Remove from the heat and stir in the broth. Return to the heat and cook, stirring, until the sauce thickens and boils. Boil for 1 minute. Remove from the heat and stir in the tarragon or dill. Add salt if necessary.

❧ Boneless Chicken Breasts with Apples

SERVES 4 TO 8, DEPENDING ON THE SIZES OF THE CHICKEN
BREASTS AND APPETITES!

Fall, or any time apples and cider are available, is a good time to
prepare this dish.

Preheat the oven to 350°F.

3 tablespoons butter or
   margarine
8 chicken breasts, skinned and
   boned (see page 187)
   Salt
½ cup chopped onion
¼ cup flour
1 cup apple cider

1 cup light cream
1 tablespoon sugar
½ teaspoon salt
¼ teaspoon nutmeg
3 medium apples (about 1
   pound), peeled and cut into
   eighths

Melt the butter in a large frying pan over medium heat. Sprinkle
the chicken breasts lightly with salt and add to the butter. Cook
until lightly browned on both sides. Remove the chicken breasts
to a shallow 9-by-13-inch baking dish. Lower the heat and add the
onion to the butter remaining in the frying pan. Cook the onion
for 2 to 3 minutes or until it softens. Remove the pan from the
heat and transfer the onion, with a slotted spoon, to the top of the
chicken. Reserve the drippings.

Place the flour in a small mixing bowl and whisk or briskly stir in
the cider. Stir in the cream. Pour this mixture into the drippings
remaining in the frying pan. Return the pan to medium-low heat
and cook, stirring, until the liquid begins to thicken. Add the sugar,
½ teaspoon salt, nutmeg, and apples. Cook for 1 minute, stirring,
until the apples are hot and coated. Spoon the apples and sauce
over the chicken. The sauce may appear to be too thick, but some
liquid will cook out of the apples and chicken in the oven. Cover
and bake at 350°F for 30 minutes. Remove the cover, turn the
chicken, and continue to cook for 15 to 20 minutes longer or
until the chicken is lightly browned. Spoon the sauce over the
chicken at least once during the uncovered cooking period.

❧ Pepper Steak

SERVES 4

1½ pounds lean beef
  4 tablespoons butter or margarine
  1 clove garlic, peeled
  3 large green peppers, seeded and sliced into ¼-inch strips (1½ pounds)
½ cup sliced scallions
1½ cups ¼-inch-sliced mushrooms

1⅓ cups Beef Broth (recipe, page 39)
  ¼ cup water
  2 tablespoons cornstarch
  2 tablespoons soy sauce
¼ to ½ teaspoon ground ginger
  Cooked rice (optional)

Slice the steak thinly into ½-by-1½-inch strips. Melt 3 tablespoons of the butter in a large frying pan. Add the steak and garlic clove. Brown the steak slightly and remove it from the pan.

Add the remaining tablespoon of butter and the sliced peppers. Sauté for 2 to 3 minutes. Add the scallions and mushrooms and continue to cook until the vegetables are slightly soft. Remove the garlic. Add the broth and simmer for 2 to 3 minutes.

Mix the water, cornstarch, and soy sauce until thoroughly blended and stir into the vegetables and broth. Stir in the ginger and return the steak to the pan. Continue to cook, stirring often, for 3 to 4 minutes or until the flavors are well blended and the sauce has thickened. Serve on rice, if desired.

NOTE: The better the quality of the steak, the better it will taste.

❧ Stuffed Flank Steak

SERVES 4 TO 6

The rather sharp flavor of the cooked chicory stuffing is not over-powered by the beef. In the spring, dandelion greens would be a good substitute. I serve it with a mushroom sauce made with the broth in which I cook the steak.

Preheat the oven to 325°F.

1½ to 2 *pounds flank steak*	¼ *cup bread crumbs*
1 *clove garlic, peeled*	¼ *teaspoon salt (or to taste)*
3 *tablespoons butter or margarine*	*Pepper to taste*
½ *cup peeled, finely chopped carrot*	3 *tablespoons oil*
½ *cup chopped onion*	1 *cup beef broth*
1½ *cups cooked, finely chopped chicory, squeezed dry*	

Score and flatten (pound) the steak to tenderize it. Cut the garlic clove in half and rub it on the side of the steak that will be covered with stuffing. Reserve the garlic. Sprinkle the same side of the steak with salt and pepper.

Melt the butter in a frying pan over medium heat. Add the chopped carrot and onion and sauté until the onion softens. Add the cooked, chopped chicory and sauté for 1 minute longer. Remove the pan from the heat and stir in the crumbs. Add salt and pepper to taste.

Spread the stuffing over the prepared steak. Pack down the stuffing slightly so it won't spill when you roll the steak. Fold in the ends and roll the steak into a long roll. Tie it with kitchen string at 2-inch intervals or fasten it carefully with skewers. Heat the oil in a large frying pan over medium-high and brown the steak on all sides. Remove the steak to a large shallow baking dish. Pour the broth over it and add the reserved garlic. Cover the pan tightly with foil. Bake at 325°F for 1½ hours or until tender. Slice into 1-inch pieces with a very sharp knife. To serve the steak with Mushroom Sauce (recipe, page 207), don't slice it until serving time.

Remove it to a platter and cover to keep it warm. Strain the liquid in the baking dish. Skim the fat and then add water, if necessary, to make 1 cup of liquid (broth). Use this liquid in place of Beef Broth in the Mushroom Sauce.

NOTE: I sometimes add other ingredients to the stuffing — for example, ⅓ cup chopped nuts, ½ cup chopped mushrooms sautéed with the onion and carrot, or 1 to 2 tablespoons crumbled blue cheese.

Mushroom Sauce

MAKES 1½ TO 2 CUPS

 2 tablespoons butter
 2 cups sliced mushrooms
 2 tablespoons flour
 1 cup Beef Broth (recipe, page 39)
 ½ teaspoon Worcestershire sauce
     Salt, if necessary
 ⅛ teaspoon freshly ground pepper

Melt the butter in a frying pan over medium heat. Add the mushrooms and sauté until they soften. Sprinkle the flour over the mushrooms and stir in the broth, Worcestershire, salt, and pepper. Cook, stirring often, for 2 to 3 minutes or until the sauce thickens. Add additional broth or water if the sauce is too thick.

Chili

SERVES 10

My chili con carne is not a traditional one. This recipe calls for ground beef (which I get from our farm in Maine), fewer beans, and less seasoning. Through the years, I've found that more people enjoy Chili this way, and you can always add more chili powder and cayenne pepper. It serves 10, but is easy to halve for a smaller number.

3 slices bacon, diced
1½ cups coarsely chopped onion
¾ cup chopped green pepper
2 pounds lean ground beef
8 cups canned red kidney beans
8 cups peeled, chopped tomatoes (seeded, if desired)

1 large clove garlic, minced
2½ teaspoons salt
1 tablespoon chili powder
⅛ to ¼ teaspoon cayenne pepper

Place the diced bacon in a heavy 6- to 8-quart pot and cook until crisp. Remove the bacon and set aside, leaving the fat in the pan. Add the onion and pepper to the bacon fat. Cook over medium heat until barely soft. Add the ground beef and continue to cook until it is brown. Add the kidney beans, tomatoes, garlic, salt, chili powder, cayenne pepper, and reserved bacon. Simmer, covered, for 15 minutes. Uncover and continue to simmer for about 35 minutes or until the tomatoes cook down. Correct the seasoning.

Beef Stew

SERVES 6 TO 8

The first time I tested to be sure of the quantities for this recipe, we weren't going to be home for dinner, so I offered it to Cindy Wilson. She accepted it eagerly (anything is better than having to cook after a long day in the farm office), saying that Jim (her husband) loves stew. When she got home, he had gone running. So she put the stew on the stove and also went running. When she returned, she found a fork in the pot and half the stew gone. I assumed that he liked it. I have made it both with and without wine, and it's good both ways. To cook it with wine, substitute 1 cup of dry red wine for 1 cup of the beef broth. Use a decent wine so you can drink the rest of the bottle with the stew.

3 pounds lean, well-trimmed
  stew meat
½ cup flour
½ teaspoon salt
⅛ teaspoon pepper
¼ cup oil
½ cup chopped onion
1 clove garlic, minced
1 cup water
3 cups Beef Broth (recipe, page 39)
1 bay leaf

½ teaspoon dried thyme
  (2 teaspoons fresh)
4 whole cloves
15 peeled, small white onions
2 cups peeled, thickly sliced carrots
3 cups peeled, ¾-inch-cubed potatoes
1 cup 1-inch pieces green beans

Cut the stew meat into 1-inch cubes. Mix the flour, salt, and pepper and flour the beef pieces thoroughly. Heat the oil in a heavy 6-quart pot. Brown the beef in the oil, a few pieces at a time, until all are brown, adding another tablespoon of oil if necessary. When all the beef cubes have been browned, return them to the pot with any remaining flour. Add the chopped onion, garlic, water, broth (or wine), bay leaf, thyme, and cloves. Place over medium heat, bring to a simmer, lower the heat, and simmer, covered, for 1¼ hours. Remove the cloves (they usually float to the surface) and bay leaf. Add the white onions, and simmer covered, for 30 minutes longer. Add the carrots, potatoes, and beans and continue to cook for about 20 minutes longer or until the vegetables are done. If you wish to thicken the stew, whisk 3 or 4 tablespoons of flour (preferably quick-mixing sauce and gravy flour) into ½ cup of water and slowly add it until the stew is the desired consistency. Cook for a few minutes longer. Correct the seasoning.

❧ Stuffed Cabbage Rolls

SERVES 8

I love Italian sausage, and, combined with mushrooms, onions, and rice, I think it's even better. I serve these cabbage rolls with a light cheese sauce, but tomato sauce is just as good. I have listed this recipe under main courses, but there is no reason why the cabbage rolls couldn't be served individually as a first course.

Preheat the oven to 350°F.

1 2- to 3-pound head green cabbage
3 cups water
6 Italian sweet sausages (or 3 sweet and 3 hot)
3 tablespoons butter or margarine
⅔ cup coarsely chopped onion

2 cups sliced mushrooms
2 cups cooked rice
Salt and pepper to taste
Wooden toothpicks
1 cup Chicken Broth (recipe, page 40)

Remove the tough outer leaves and the core from the cabbage and wash it thoroughly. Bring the water to a boil in a 4-quart pot. Place the cabbage in the water, cored side down, and blanch until the leaves soften and pull away (about 10 minutes). Run the cabbage under cold water to stop the cooking process and separate the leaves — you'll need about 18. Set the leaves aside and make the stuffing.

Remove the casing from the sausages and break them into small pieces. Cook the sausage meat in a frying pan until it's no longer pink. Drain and set aside.

Melt the butter in a large frying pan. Add the onion, sauté for 1 to 2 minutes, then add the mushrooms. Continue to sauté until the onions and mushrooms soften. Combine the rice, sausage meat, mushrooms, and onions (and any liquid in the pan), and salt and pepper.

Make the cabbage rolls by placing 3 to 4 tablespoons of the stuffing in the center of a cabbage leaf, fold in the sides, and roll. Secure with toothpicks. Place, seam side down, in two shallow 8-inch-square baking dishes or one very large shallow dish. Pour ½ cup of the chicken broth into each dish and cover tightly with foil. Bake at 350°F for 40 to 45 minutes. Remove the toothpicks. Serve with cheese or tomato sauce.

Cheese Sauce for Cabbage Rolls

2 tablespoons butter or
    margarine
2 tablespoons flour
1¼ cups milk

1 cup grated or diced medium
    sharp cheddar cheese
½ teaspoon dry mustard
Salt and pepper to taste

Melt the butter in a 2-quart saucepan. Stir in the flour and cook over medium-low heat until bubbly. Stir in the milk and continue to cook, stirring, until it comes to a boil. Cook for 1 minute longer. Add the cheese, mustard, and salt and pepper and stir until the cheese melts. Pour over the cabbage rolls.

❧ Stuffed Green Peppers

I prefer sausage to ground beef in my rice stuffing. Although they are included as a main course, I serve the peppers as a vegetable side dish with a light meal. Whether as a main course or a side dish, they are always warmly welcomed at the farm. Vinnie Greeno, who is our expert on Italian cooking and loves sausages, threatened to tell me that they needed improvement so I would test them several more times.

Preheat the oven to 350°F.

6 small (4 large) green peppers	3 sweet Italian sausages, cooked and thinly sliced
4 tablespoons butter or margarine	1½ cups lightly packed cooked rice
2 tablespoons chopped green pepper	⅔ cup peeled, chopped tomato
¼ cup chopped onion	Salt and pepper to taste
1 teaspoon finely minced garlic	¾ cup water, broth, or tomato juice
⅔ cup coarsely chopped ¼-inch pieces mushrooms	1 tablespoon grated Parmesan cheese (optional)

Cut off the tops and remove the seeds from the peppers. Blanch them in boiling water for 5 minutes. Remove from the water, drain well, and let cool slightly.

For the stuffing, melt 2 tablespoons of the butter in a large frying pan. Add the 2 tablespoons of chopped green pepper, and the onion, garlic, and mushrooms and sauté over medium heat until soft. Add the cooked sausages, rice, remaining 2 tablespoons of butter, tomato, and salt and pepper. Cook for 1 to 2 minutes or until heated through.

Fill the peppers with the stuffing. Place in a shallow baking dish. Add the liquid (water, broth, or juice) to a depth of ½ inch. Cover loosely with foil. Bake, covered, at 350°F for 20 minutes. Uncover and sprinkle the top of each pepper with a little cheese, and bake for 15 to 20 minutes longer.

❧ Broccoli and Ham with Cheese Sauce

SERVES 6

Broccoli, ham, and cheese make a good combination. It's a great dish for a buffet table, since it may be doubled easily and made the day before a party. It's just as good without the ham, but if you use it, buy a chunk of unsliced ham, and cut it into ½-inch cubes.

Preheat the oven to 375°F. Butter a shallow 2-quart casserole.

1 to 1½ pounds broccoli
2 cups milk
4 tablespoons butter or margarine
3 tablespoons flour
1½ cups shredded Swiss cheese

2 tablespoons grated Parmesan or Romano cheese
Salt and pepper to taste
¾ pound cooked ham, cut into ½-inch cubes (about 2 cups)

Wash and trim the broccoli. Split the large florets into smaller ones. Steam or cook the broccoli in boiling, salted water for 5 minutes or until barely tender. Drain very well and chop into 1-inch pieces.

Heat the milk. Melt the butter over medium-low heat in a 2-quart saucepan and stir in the flour until blended. Pour in the hot milk. Return to the heat and cook over medium heat, stirring, until the mixture thickens and comes to a boil. Boil for 1 minute and remove from the heat. Stir in 1 cup of the Swiss cheese and the Parmesan cheese. Continue to stir until the cheese melts. Season to taste with salt and pepper and set aside. Spread half the broccoli in the prepared casserole. Top with half the cubed ham and half the cheese sauce. Repeat the layers and sprinkle the top of the casserole with the remaining ½ cup of Swiss cheese.

Bake, uncovered, at 375°F for about 30 minutes or until lightly browned and bubbly.

NOTE: This dish may be fully prepared, covered, and refrigerated a day in advance. Adjust the baking time if the casserole is cold. Be careful not to oversalt the cheese sauce because the ham may be salty.

❦ Des Moines (Acorn) Squash Stuffed with Sour Cream and Sausage

SERVES 4

This combination sounds strange but tastes great! I usually use breakfast sausage links, but sweet Italian sausage does just as well.

Preheat the oven to 350°F.

2 acorn squash (1 to 1½ pound each)
¾ pound sausage links
1½ tablespoons butter or margarine

2 cups coarsely chopped mushrooms
⅔ cup chopped onion
½ cup sour cream
Salt and pepper to taste

Cut the squash in half and remove the seeds. Place the halves, cut side down, in ½ inch of hot water in a shallow pan. Bake at 350°F until the squash is soft — about 45 minutes.

While the squash is cooking, cook the sausage, cut it into ½-inch pieces, and set aside. Sauté the mushrooms and onion in the butter until soft. Set aside.

When the squash is done, scoop it out of the skin, being careful not to damage it. Mix the pulp with the sour cream, sausage, mushrooms, onions, and any remaining butter. Add salt and pepper. Fill the skins with the mixture, place them in a shallow baking dish, and bake at 350°F for 20 to 25 minutes. If necessary, brown the tops under the broiler.

Scallops with Broccoli and Noodles

SERVES 6 TO 8

The only problem I find with this recipe is that it uses too many pans. However, pan-washing is quickly forgotten when you sit down to eat.

Preheat the oven to 350°F. Butter a deep 2½- or 3-quart casserole.

2½ to 3 cups broccoli florets
⅓ pound uncooked medium egg noodles
5 tablespoons butter or margarine
⅓ cup sliced scallions
½ cup diced red pepper (or ¼ cup green)
¾ pound bay scallops
3 tablespoons sherry
1 tablespoon lemon juice
⅓ cup flour
1½ cups milk
1 cup light cream
1 teaspoon salt
⅛ teaspoon pepper
½ cup shredded Swiss cheese (optional)

Wash and steam or blanch the broccoli florets until barely tender (about 4 minutes). Drain and set aside.

Cook the noodles in boiling, salted water until tender but not overdone. Drain well and set aside.

Place 2 tablespoons of the butter in a large frying pan. Add the scallions and chopped pepper and sauté for 1 to 2 minutes. Add the scallops (cut large ones in half) and continue to cook for 2 to 3 minutes. Add the sherry and lemon juice and cook for 1 minute longer. Remove from the heat and set aside.

Melt the remaining 3 tablespoons of butter in a saucepan and stir in the flour. Blend in the milk and cream with a wire whisk. Cook until the sauce comes to a boil and thickens. Simmer for 1 minute and remove from the heat. Stir in the salt and pepper. Mix the sauce with the broccoli, scallop mixture (with any liquid), and noodles. Correct the seasoning. Spoon into the prepared casserole and top with the cheese. Bake, uncovered, at 350°F for 20 to 30 minutes or until the sauce is bubbly and the cheese melts.

❧Lamb Shish Kebab

Many years ago, an Armenian friend of my sister-in-law told her to marinate lamb for shish kebab in tomato sauce, oil, vinegar, and onions. It was so delicious that we have both done that ever since. When I was deciding what to include in the main-course chapter, Barbara reminded me of shish kebab. I usually serve it during the summer, cooked on a grill. However, it may be broiled in the oven.

2 large (3 medium) yellow onions
1 29-ounce can tomato sauce
1 clove garlic, peeled and minced
1 tablespoon vinegar
2 tablespoons oil
2 pounds trimmed, cubed lamb (1- to 1½-inch pieces)

1 to 2 pounds mushrooms, trimmed
4 large red or green peppers, or 2 of each
1 to 2 pints cherry tomatoes (or 4 to 6 firm tomatoes, cut into quarters)
Salt to taste

Peel the onions, cut them into quarters, and separate the quarters into pieces. Mix the onions, tomato sauce, garlic, vinegar, oil, and lamb in a large stainless-steel or glass bowl. Cover and marinate in the refrigerator overnight (or for at least 8 hours).

Add the mushrooms to the marinade at least 1 hour before cooking. Stir to coat the mushrooms. Cut the peppers into eighths.

Place the mushrooms, peppers, tomatoes, onions, and lamb on the skewers, alternating them. Brush the skewers with marinade and sprinkle with salt. Broil, turning often, until done (about 10 minutes). Brush with marinade or melted butter while cooking, if desired. Serve with Rice Pilaf (recipe follows), Syrian pocket bread, and salad.

Rice Pilaf

A good complement to shish kebab, Rice Pilaf is very simple to make and may be prepared ahead and reheated in the oven.

⅓ cup butter
¼ cup chopped onion
⅔ cup uncooked fine egg noodles
1 cup long-grain rice

2 cups Chicken Broth (recipe, page 40)
⅓ cup lightly browned pine nuts (optional)
Salt to taste

Melt the butter in a 2-quart saucepan over medium heat. Add the onion and sauté for 1 minute. Add the noodles and cook until they are brown. Stir in the rice until it is coated with butter. Add the broth, cover, and bring to a simmer. Simmer, covered, until the broth is absorbed. Add the pine nuts (pignolias) and salt, if necessary, after cooking.

✿ Eggplant Parmigiana

SERVES 4 TO 6

I appreciate the taste of eggplant, so I'm often disappointed, when I order this dish in a restaurant, to find that the slices are paper thin. If you slice the eggplant $\frac{1}{3}$ inch thick, its flavor won't be overpowered by the tomato and cheese. Use the recipe for Fresh Tomato Sauce, which follows, to prepare this dish.

Preheat the oven to 350°F.

1 to 1½ pounds eggplant	½ teaspoon salt
2 eggs	⅛ teaspoon pepper
1 tablespoon water	Oil
¾ cup bread crumbs	Fresh Tomato Sauce
¼ cup grated Parmesan cheese	⅔ pound mozzarella cheese, shredded

Peel and slice the eggplant.

Beat the eggs and water together and place them in a shallow dish. Mix the crumbs, Parmesan cheese, salt, and pepper and place them in another shallow dish. Dip the eggplant slices in the egg, then in the crumb mixture, coating both sides.

Heat a small amount of oil (about ⅛ inch deep) in a large frying pan over medium. Add the coated eggplant slices and fry, turning once, until brown on both sides. Drain on paper towels.

Place two layers of Tomato Sauce, eggplant, and mozzarella cheese, in that order, in a shallow 2-quart baking dish. Bake, uncovered, at 350°F for 20 to 30 minutes or until the sauce is bubbly and the cheese melts.

❧ Fresh Tomato Sauce

MAKES 5 TO 6 CUPS

My Tomato Sauce is unlike the traditional one, which always took seemingly forever to cook. Although it takes less than an hour, our daughter, Lesley, who much prefers tomato sauce to meat sauce, says it is "wicked good." It tastes like fresh tomatoes and is fine on spaghetti, veal, chicken, and, of course, eggplant.

8 cups peeled, seeded, chopped
ripe tomatoes (8 to 10)
3 tablespoons oil
1/3 cup finely chopped onion
1 clove garlic, peeled and finely
minced (1 to 1 1/2 teaspoons)

1/4 teaspoon dried oregano
(about 1 teaspoon if fresh)
3 tablespoons chopped fresh
basil
1 teaspoon salt
1/4 teaspoon sugar

Peel, seed, and chop enough tomatoes to make 8 cups. Set aside.

Heat the oil in a 4-quart pot. Add the onion and garlic and sauté over medium heat until soft. Add the tomatoes, oregano, basil, salt, and sugar. Cover and simmer for 15 minutes. Remove the cover, raise the heat slightly, and cook, uncovered, stirring occasionally, until thick — 30 to 45 minutes. Correct the seasoning.

NOTE: If you don't use all the sauce for a particular dish, refrigerate the remainder for another day.

❧Ziti with Vegetables

SERVES APPROXIMATELY 8

This is a good vegetarian dish for lunch or dinner and also makes a different appetizer. I make it with ziti, rotini, or one of the other large macaronis rather than spaghetti.

1 pound ziti or other pasta	3 tablespoons butter or margarine
2 to 3 cups broccoli florets	1 clove garlic, peeled and cut in half
2 cups summer squash (¾ pound, seeded)	½ teaspoon salt (or to taste)
2 cups peeled, seeded, ½-inch pieces ripe tomatoes	¼ teaspoon ground pepper
1 tablespoon chopped parsley	⅓ cup grated Romano or Parmesan cheese
2 tablespoons oil	

Cook the pasta in boiling, salted water until done.

While the pasta is cooking, steam the broccoli until crisp-tender (about 4 minutes).

Cut the squash into quarters lengthwise, removing most of the seeds, and then into ½-inch chunks. Peel, seed, and chop the tomatoes. Chop the parsley.

Heat the oil and butter in a large frying pan with the cut clove of garlic. Add the squash and sauté until it begins to soften (3 to 4 minutes). Remove the garlic and add the cooked broccoli. Sauté for 1 minute. Add the tomatoes and parsley and sauté for 1 minute longer or until the tomatoes are hot. Drain the pasta well and place it in a large, heated bowl. Add the contents of the frying pan, salt, pepper, and cheese. Toss until well mixed. Serve immediately.

❧ Pesto

MAKES ¾ TO 1 CUP

Pesto, a sauce made with fresh basil, garlic, oil, and cheese, is wonderful served on spaghetti or any other pasta, and a spoonful
added to soup or potato salad gives a delightful flavor. The old-
fashioned method of making pesto was with a mortar and pestle.
However, that is very time-consuming, and I find it much easier to
do it in my blender.

2 cups lightly packed fresh
  basil leaves
¼ cup fresh Italian (flat-leaf)
  parsley
¼ cup pine nuts (pignolias)
2 cloves garlic, peeled

⅓ cup grated Parmesan cheese
½ teaspoon salt
½ cup olive oil
1 tablespoon butter

Place all the ingredients in a blender. Purée until the sauce is
smooth, pushing down the basil leaves as necessary. When you use
the sauce on pasta, reserve ¼ cup of the pasta cooking water before draining. Use all or part of this water, together with the pesto,
for the sauce. When you mix the pesto sauce with the pasta, stir
in enough of the reserved cooking water to provide the proper
consistency.

NOTE: This amount of sauce is adequate to coat at least ¾ pound
of pasta. Pesto may be refrigerated for a week but should be covered with a thin film of olive oil to prevent discoloration.

Desserts

*A*h, Desserts! . . . *the longest chapter* with the most recipes. Does this tell you something about my rather rotund figure? The employees at the farm love anything sweet, so when I was testing these recipes I didn't get many negative comments. As a matter of fact, people who claimed they never eat dessert were happy to sample these. If it was sweet, it was popular. Those who wouldn't touch parsnips as a vegetable loved them in pie. Fruit desserts are always popular, but even when I used such vegetables as winter squash or zucchini, carrots, or parsnips in pies and cakes, everyone wanted a taste.

When I make desserts and breads with vegetables (for example, parsnips, squash, pumpkin), I always use the fresh varieties. It isn't difficult to cook them, and the difference in flavor is well worth the effort. I whip the cooked, well-drained vegetable until smooth with an electric mixer to take out the lumps but leave some texture. A potato masher seems to leave too many lumps, and puréeing in a blender or food processor makes the vegetable too smooth for my taste. Cooked squash, pumpkin, and parsnips freeze beautifully, so I often freeze extra for future baked items. Be sure to drain vegetables very well so pies won't be wet.

Small, dark orange sugar pumpkins are best for cooking. They usually weigh 3 to 5 pounds and yield approximately ¾ cup of cooked pumpkin per pound. Any winter squash (butternut, Hubbard, turban) is fine.

Fruit desserts, from the simplest slice of melon or bowl of cut-up fruit to the most complicated pie, are always a hit. As with my other recipes, I've attempted to provide easy-to-make desserts. Some may take more time than others to prepare, but none is very difficult. As you read through the recipes, you'll notice that because I tend to be a "last minute" person who often has unexpected company, I frequently make desserts that can be served warm and topped with ice cream.

Since you generally don't use much in the way of spices when you cook with fruit, the end product depends on the quality and flavor of the fruit. If possible, always use ripe, locally grown fruit in season. I'm not saying that you shouldn't make strawberry shortcake in December just because there are no local berries around. Fresh strawberries and other fruits are now available practically year round. However, if you live in the Northeast, your shortcake won't be quite as good in December as in June, when you can make it with freshly picked strawberries.

The fruits I use in these recipes are all grown in New England as well as in other parts of the country. Naturally, the seasons and varieties depend on the climate. Florida and California ship vegetables and fruits all year, and other states have a longer growing season than New England. In the Northeast, the season for fresh fruit begins in spring with rhubarb and continues through the winter months with storage apples. I have listed below the major fruit crops of this area in order of their times of harvest.

Rhubarb

A sure sign of spring is the appearance of rhubarb about the end of April. It is available until the end of June. Rhubarb, which is easy to freeze, can sometimes be found in frozen food cases when it is out of season.

Strawberries

The New England crop is harvested from early June to early July, depending on the weather. Some of our favorite varieties are Raritan, Honeoye, and Guardian. The Honeoye are on the tart side, while the others are very sweet.

Blueberries

Large cultivated blueberries are available from the beginning of July until the end of August, depending on the variety and the area in which they are grown. I use these blueberries for pancakes, coffee cakes, muffins, and with cream and sugar. But for pie, I prefer the small, wild blueberries, which have such a lovely sweet flavor. Depending on where you live, you can find them at your store or local farm stand from the Fourth of July until almost Labor Day.

Raspberries

Raspberries are a delicacy with just cream and sugar. We grow two early varieties — Taylor, which is quite sweet, and Brandywine, which is tart and ideal for jams and jellies. Both are harvested in early July. The later varieties, Heritage and Amity, produce sweet, flavorful berries from mid-August into early October.

Blackberries

Blackberries ripen in midsummer, but there still aren't many available despite their increasing popularity. Years ago, they grew wild near our home in Lexington. As children, we used to pick them, and my mother made delicious blackberry cobbler. Now when I have them, I usually serve them with cream and sugar. Since the demand for blackberries is increasing, I'm sure there will be a greater supply in the future.

Peaches

Many varieties of peaches are grown in the Northeast — Sun Haven, Red Haven, Sunhigh, Blakes, Lorings. I could go on and on. The local season starts in August and continues through September. My favorite desserts are made with peaches, which I peel with a knife. However, you can dip them in boiling water for 5 to 10 seconds to make peeling easier (as you do tomatoes). Make sure they don't cook, because they become mushy if they do.

Pears

Many pears are shipped into New England from other states, so they are available almost all year. The most popular local varieties are Clapp in late August, Bartlett in mid-September, and Bosc, which are harvested from late September through early October. The small, sweet Seckel pears, which are sometimes used for canning but are also delightful raw, are on the market in late August.

Apples

A major crop in the Northeast, apples start in late August and, because several varieties are stored in controlled atmosphere storage through the winter, good local apples are available into the spring. Although many kinds are grown, the most important varieties are red Delicious, golden Delicious, Empire, Cortland, Macintosh, Macoun, Paula Red, and Rome. Most cooks have their favorites, and I'm no exception. I definitely prefer Cortlands, although, when I can get them, I use Gravensteins, an old-fashioned, less popular, early variety.

Cranberries

The last major crop to be harvested before winter, fresh cranberries are available from the end of September through Christmas. They can be frozen whole for use during the rest of the year, and are sometimes seen in the frozen food section, so you can serve your favorite cranberry dish in the spring as well as in the fall.

Plums

Some plums, mainly Santa Rosa and prune plums, are grown in the Northeast, but the crop is not substantial.

Melons

Many muskmelons — rough-skinned native cantaloupes — are grown for local consumption and are available late in August. Incidentally, I think that melons at room temperature have more flavor than chilled melons.

The following recipes include ingredients that have to be prepared in advance, so it might be a good idea to read all of the ingredients before beginning a recipe. For instance, butter may have to be softened and squash cooked. I use dark, rather than light, brown sugar because it gives a stronger flavor, but light brown is quite acceptable. Unless a recipe specifies brown sugar, use white, granulated sugar. Spices are ground unless otherwise stated. I suggest whipped cream as a topping for many of these desserts, so you will find my recipe for it on page 264.

Have fun! I hope you enjoy trying these recipes as much as the farm crew enjoyed testing them.

❧ Pastry for a 9-inch Single-Crust Pie

1¼ cups flour
¾ teaspoon salt
6½ tablespoons solid vegetable
   shortening

3 to 4 tablespoons ice water
   (more or less)

Using a fork, stir the flour and salt together. Cut in the shortening with a pastry blender or two knives until the mixture resembles very coarse cornmeal. Stir in the ice water with a fork, a tablespoon at a time, until the pastry holds together. Press into a ball. Chill for 30 minutes. Roll out on a lightly floured surface and place in a pie plate. I roll it up on a rolling pin and then unroll it over the pie plate. If you prefer, fold the crust in half and place it in the pie plate. Fit the pastry loosely into the pie plate and trim the edges.

NOTE: Some recipes call for an unbaked pie shell, others, for pre-baked. See specific directions for each recipe.

❧ Pastry for a 9-inch Two-Crust Pie

2 cups flour
1 teaspoon salt
¾ cup solid vegetable
   shortening

5 tablespoons ice water (more
   or less)

Using a fork, stir the flour and salt together. Cut in the shortening with a pastry blender or two knives until the mixture resembles very coarse cornmeal. Stir in the ice water with a fork, a tablespoon at a time, until the pastry holds together. Press into a ball. Chill for 30 minutes. Divide the dough in half and roll out on a lightly floured surface, making the bottom crust slightly thicker than the top. Fit the bottom pastry loosely into a pie plate and trim the edges almost even with the rim. Set the top crust aside and follow the directions in the individual recipes.

NOTE: Some recipes call for an unbaked pie shell, others, for pre-baked. See specific directions for each recipe.

✲ Graham Cracker Crust

1¼ cups graham cracker crumbs
¼ cup sugar
5 tablespoons butter or
  margarine, melted

¼ teaspoon nutmeg or
  cinnamon (optional)

Blend all the ingredients thoroughly in a mixing bowl. Turn the mixture into a 9- or 10-inch pie plate and pack firmly to make the shell.

NOTE: Some recipes call for an unbaked pie shell, others, for pre-baked. See specific directions for each recipe. If the pie shell is to be prebaked, bake it at 400°F for 7 to 8 minutes unless otherwise specified in the recipe.

❧ Fruit Cobbler

SERVES 6 TO 8

My mother often served what she called a cobbler. Made of fruit with pastry on both bottom and top, it is baked in a deep casserole. I've since learned that a cobbler has biscuit dough on top. However, like Mom, I also make deep-dish pies, which my family refers to as cobblers. They taste like pie, but take less time to make, as you have to roll out only one crust. Since you spoon it into a bowl, you don't have to be too fussy. It doesn't matter whether the crust is perfect, or the filling has exactly the right amount of flour, or you make it at the last minute and it's still very warm.

This pastry can also be used for a 10-inch single-crust pie.

CRUST

1½ cups flour
1¼ teaspoons salt
½ cup solid vegetable shortening

2 to 3 tablespoons ice water

Using a fork, stir the flour and salt together. Cut in the shortening with a pastry blender or two knives until the mixture is between the size of cornmeal and oatmeal. Stir in 2 tablespoons of the ice water with a fork, adding more water only if necessary. Press into a ball. Roll out on a lightly floured surface. Fit the pastry into a deep 1½- or 2-quart casserole, leaving the edges hanging out over the sides.

FILLING

See the recipes for Peach Pie (page 237), Blueberry Pie (page 234), or Strawberry-Rhubarb Pie (page 232).

Fill the shell with the amount of fruit required for a 9-inch pie, dot the top with butter cut into small pieces, and flop the pastry over to cover the top of the fruit. If it doesn't quite cover the filling, no problem. It still tastes wonderful. Bake the cobbler according to the directions in the fruit pie recipes. Spoon it into individual bowls and top with ice cream.

❧ Rhubarb Pie

My mother, who makes good pie, always puts an egg in her rhubarb pie. Of course, being a typical daughter, I thought if one egg was good, then two or three should be better. Well, I tried it, and, as usual, Mother knows best, so here is a rhubarb pie recipe using one egg.

Preheat the oven to 425°F.

CRUST

Prepare enough pastry for an unbaked two-crust pie (recipe, page 228). Use a 10-inch, or very deep 9-inch, pie plate, as rhubarb tends to boil over and make a mess of the oven!

FILLING

1 egg, beaten	1 tablespoon butter or
1¾ cups sugar	margarine
½ cup flour	
¼ teaspoon cinnamon	
5 to 6 cups ½-inch pieces rhubarb (about 2 pounds)	

Blend the beaten egg, sugar, flour, and cinnamon in a large mixing bowl. The mixture should resemble cornmeal. Add the rhubarb and stir. Fill the bottom crust with the rhubarb mixture. Dot the filling with the butter, cut into small pieces. Roll out the top crust and cover. Make sure the edges are well sealed. Cut steam vents. Bake at 425°F for about 45 minutes or until the crust is brown and the filling starts to bubble through the vents. Serve slightly warm.

❧ Strawberry-Rhubarb Pie

Preheat the oven to 425°F.

CRUST

Make enough pastry for an unbaked two-crust pie (recipe, page 228). Place the bottom crust in a deep 9-inch pie plate.

FILLING

1 pint strawberries, halved
(2 to 3 cups)
3 cups ½-inch-sliced rhubarb
(about 1 pound)
1⅓ cups sugar

½ cup flour
¼ teaspoon cinnamon
1 tablespoon butter or
margarine

Gently mix the strawberries, rhubarb, sugar, flour, and cinnamon. Spoon into the bottom crust and dot with the butter, cut into small pieces. Roll out the top crust and cover the pie. Seal carefully and cut steam vents. Bake at 425°F for about 45 minutes or until the crust is brown and the filling starts to bubble through the vents. Serve slightly warm with ice cream.

NOTE: If the rhubarb is very thick, cut it lengthwise before slicing.

❧ Strawberry Bavarian Cream Pie

This is my husband's and son's favorite pie. Of course, they don't agree on the ideal crust. Alan wants regular pastry and Scott likes graham cracker. Whichever crust, this pie is so popular that I don't bother to make strawberry chiffon anymore. This recipe is really not complicated, but it has to be done in several steps.

CRUST

Prepare and prebake a 9-inch pie shell (recipes, pages 228 and 229) — either pastry (at 375°F for 12 minutes) or graham cracker crumb (at 400°F for 7 to 8 minutes). Cool before filling.

FILLING

¾ quart strawberries (about 3 cups)
⅓ cup sugar (or sweeten to taste)
1 envelope unflavored gelatin
½ cup sugar
1 cup heavy cream

Mash the strawberries with a fork or potato masher, and add the ⅓ cup of sugar. Let stand until the sugar dissolves and the juices (syrup) form — 5 to 10 minutes. Strain the berries, separating them from the juice. You will need 1 cup of juice (add water to make 1 cup, if necessary) and 1 cup of mashed berries without much liquid. Reserve any unused berries for future use. Combine ¼ cup of the strawberry juice with the gelatin. Let stand for 5 minutes or until the gelatin softens.

Pour the remaining strawberry juice (¾ cup) into a small saucepan and bring to a simmer over low heat. Remove from the heat and stir in the ½ cup of sugar and the gelatin mixture. Stir until the sugar and gelatin are dissolved. Pour into a mixing bowl and chill until partially set, stirring occasionally.

When partially set, beat with an eggbeater until smooth. Stir in 1 cup mashed strawberries. Set aside.

Whip the cream until stiff and fold into the strawberry-gelatin mixture. Pour into the cooled, baked pie shell. Chill at least 3 hours or until firm.

Top with whipped cream before serving, if desired.

NOTE: Leftover pie should be refrigerated.

❧ Blueberry Pie

The farm crew always stops work when I come through with blueberry pie. I have to cut it into tiny pieces so everyone gets a taste. I don't like tart pie, so I seldom put lemon juice in mine.

Preheat the oven to 425°F.

CRUST

Make enough pastry for an unbaked two-crust pie (recipe, page 228) or cobbler (recipe, page 230).

FILLING

1 quart wild blueberries
(4 to 5 cups)
²⁄₃ cup sugar
¹⁄₃ cup flour
¹⁄₄ teaspoon cinnamon

1 to 2 teaspoons lemon juice
(optional)
1 tablespoon butter or
margarine

Mix the blueberries, sugar, flour, cinnamon, and lemon juice. Spoon into the bottom pie crust and dot with the butter, cut into small pieces. Cover with the top crust and seal carefully. Cut steam vents and bake at 425°F for approximately 40 minutes or until the crust is brown and the juice starts to bubble through the vents. Serve slightly warm with ice cream.

❧ Raspberry and Cream Pie

Once in a while, Joanie Simmons, who's worked at the farm for many years, likes something I've made so much that she says, "That was so good that I thought I'd died and gone to heaven." This is the ultimate compliment, and I always anxiously await her reaction to new recipes. Anyway, here's a recipe for Joanie and my other friends who believe that raspberries, sugar, and cream are heavenly.

Prcheat the oven to 400°F.

CRUST

Prepare an unbaked 9-inch pie shell (recipe, page 228).

FILLING

½ cup flour	Dash cinnamon
1 cup sugar (¾ cup if raspberries are very sweet)	4 cups fresh raspberries
1¼ cups heavy cream	

Blend the flour, sugar, cream, and cinnamon with a wire whisk or fork. Put the raspberries in a large mixing bowl and pour the cream mixture over them. Stir gently to coat the raspberries. Spoon the raspberries and cream mixture into the pie shell. Bake at 400°F for approximately 40 minutes or until set. Serve at room temperature or slightly chilled.

NOTE: Leftover pie should be refrigerated.

❧ Cheese Pie with Raspberry Glaze

Remove the cream cheese from the refrigerator at least 2 hours before starting this recipe.

Preheat the oven to 325°F.

CRUST

Prepare an unbaked 9-inch graham cracker crust (recipe, page 229).

FILLING

1 pound cream cheese, softened	3 eggs
²/₃ cup sugar	1¹/₄ teaspoons vanilla

Beat the cream cheese with an electric mixer until smooth. Gradually beat in the sugar and then the eggs, one at a time. When the mixture is very smooth, blend in the vanilla. Pour the mixture into the pie shell and bake at 325°F until set — about 40 minutes. Remove from the oven and chill for about 2 hours before topping with the raspberry glaze.

GLAZE

1¹/₂ teaspoons unflavored gelatin	¹/₂ cup sugar
5 tablespoons cold water	Dash nutmeg
2¹/₂ to 3 cups raspberries	

Mix the gelatin and 2 tablespoons of the cold water. Set aside to soften the gelatin. Mash 1¹/₂ cups of the raspberries slightly, with a fork, and place in a small saucepan with the remaining 3 tablespoons of water. Simmer over low heat until very soft. Remove from the heat and press through a sieve, reserving the juice. Discard the seeds and pulp. Return the juice to the saucepan and add the sugar, gelatin mixture, and nutmeg. Cook over low heat until the gelatin and sugar are dissolved.

Chill until thickened but not firm, stirring occasionally. Gently stir the remaining 1 to 1¹/₂ cups of raspberries into the glaze. Spoon the coated raspberries on top of the chilled pie. Pour the remaining glaze over the pie if needed. Chill until firm, about two additional hours.

❧ Peach Pie

This recipe makes a two-crust pie or a cobbler. I can't resist peach pie still warm from the oven with a touch of vanilla ice cream. When I make peach cobbler, I sometimes garnish it with light cream instead of ice cream.

Preheat the oven to 425°F.

CRUST

Prepare enough pastry for an unbaked two-crust pie (recipe, page 228). Place the bottom crust in a 9-inch pie plate.

FILLING

5 cups peeled, sliced peaches	1/4 teaspoon cinnamon
1 cup sugar	1 tablespoon butter or margarine
1/3 to 1/2 cup flour (1/2 cup for juicy peaches)	

Mix the peaches, sugar, flour, and cinnamon. Spoon into the bottom crust and dot with the butter, cut into small pieces. Cover with the top pastry and seal carefully. Cut steam vents and bake at 425°F for approximately 45 minutes or until the crust is brown and the peaches start to bubble through the vents. Serve slightly warm with ice cream.

 Open Peach-Almond Pie

Somehow, peaches and almonds make a nice combination. I think that any peach dessert is delicious, but if you don't like almond flavor, just eliminate it and you have peach cream pie.

Preheat the oven to 400°F.

CRUST

Prepare enough pastry for an unbaked 9-inch pie shell (recipe, page 228).

FILLING

3½ *cups peeled and sliced*
   peaches
⅔ *cup sugar*
⅓ *cup flour*
⅛ *teaspoon nutmeg*

1 *cup heavy cream*
⅛ *teaspoon almond flavoring*
⅓ *cup slivered almonds*

Mix the peaches, sugar, flour, and nutmeg and place in the pie shell. Blend the cream and almond flavoring and pour them over the peaches. Bake at 400°F until set — about 35 minutes. Remove from the oven and sprinkle with the slivered almonds. Return to the oven and bake for 5 minutes more. Serve at room temperature or chilled.

NOTE: Leftover pie should be refrigerated.

Peach Cheese Pie

SERVES 10 TO 12

Glazed or not, this is a superb dessert. Our daughter, who loves cheese pie and thinks anything made with peaches is excellent, claims that this is an unbeatable combination. Use fresh, ripe peaches for the best flavor.

Preheat the oven to 400°F.

CRUST

Prepare a 10-inch graham cracker crust (recipe, page 229), adding ¼ teaspoon ground nutmeg to the crumbs. Bake the crust at 400°F for 6 minutes. Remove from the oven and let cool slightly before filling.

Turn down the oven to 350°F.

FILLING

1 pound cream cheese, softened
2 eggs
¼ cup flour
1 cup sugar (less for very sweet peaches)

1½ cups peeled and mashed peaches (leave some texture; see Note)
2 tablespoons peach brandy (optional)

Using an electric mixer, beat the cream cheese until smooth. Add the eggs, one at a time, beating after each addition until very smooth. Beat in the flour, then gradually beat in the sugar. Stir in the mashed peaches and the brandy. Pour the mixture into the crust. Bake at 350°F for about 45 minutes or until set. Cool and top with peach glaze.

NOTE: If peaches are very ripe, you can simply mash them with a potato masher or fork. If you use a blender or food processor, be careful not to overmash. You don't want a thin purée for this pie.

PEACH GLAZE (OPTIONAL)

2 tablespoons cornstarch
½ cup peach jam

½ cup water
3 peaches, peeled and sliced

Mix the cornstarch, jam, and water in a 2-quart saucepan. Bring to a boil over medium heat, stirring constantly. Boil for about 2 minutes, stirring, until the mixture appears less cloudy. Be careful not to burn it. Remove the pan from the heat and stir in the peaches. Return to the heat and cook the peaches until they begin to soften — 2 to 3 minutes. Again, make sure it doesn't burn. Remove from the heat and cool to lukewarm. Using a fork, arrange the peach slices on the pie. Spoon the glaze over the top of the pie to cover lightly. Refrigerate the pie until chilled.

ᔒ Apple Pie

I use Cortland apples for pie when they are available because even cooked ones hold their shape. If you like a pie filling that is more like applesauce, use Macintosh. Everyone has a favorite cooking apple, so adjust the amount of sugar and baking time to suit yours. In this recipe, for example, Cortlands need ½ cup of sugar and tart apples 1 cup. Apples that have been in storage for several months have to bake a while longer.

Preheat the oven to 425°F.

CRUST

Prepare enough pastry for an unbaked two-crust 9-inch pie (recipe, page 228).

FILLING

7 cups peeled, cored, and sliced apples (about 2 pounds)	¼ teaspoon nutmeg 1 tablespoon butter or margarine
½ to 1 cup sugar	
½ teaspoon cinnamon	

Mix the apples, sugar, and spices. Spoon into the bottom pie shell and dot with the butter, cut into small pieces. Cover the pie with the top crust, sealing carefully. Cut steam vents. Bake at 425°F for about 50 minutes or until the crust is brown and the apples soft.

❧ Apple Custard Pie

I know that many people may be horrified, but I truly prefer a custard to a standard apple pie. At any rate, it is a pleasant change for anyone.

Preheat the oven to 400°F.

CRUST

Prepare enough pastry for an unbaked 9-inch pie shell (recipe, page 228).

FILLING

4 cups peeled, cored, and thinly sliced apples (1 pound makes a scant 4 cups, which is adequate)
½ cup sugar (more for very tart apples)
2 teaspoons lemon juice

¼ teaspoon cinnamon
¼ teaspoon nutmeg
2 eggs
1 cup light cream
1½ tablespoons sugar
¼ teaspoon cinnamon

Mix the apples, ½ cup of sugar, lemon juice, cinnamon, and nutmeg. Spoon the mixture into the pie shell. Arrange the apple slices so they are evenly distributed. Cover the pie loosely with foil and bake at 400°F for 20 minutes.

While the pie is baking, beat the eggs and cream. After 20 minutes, remove the foil from the pie and pour the eggs and cream over the apples. Continue to bake, uncovered, for 15 minutes longer. Mix the 1½ tablespoons of sugar and ¼ teaspoon cinnamon and sprinkle over the top of the pie. Bake for 5 minutes longer or until the custard is set. The pie should bake a total of about 40 minutes. Serve at room temperature or chilled.

NOTE: Leftover pie should be refrigerated.

❧ Cranberry-Pear Streusel Pie

Preheat the oven to 400°F.

CRUST

Prepare an unbaked 10-inch pie shell (recipe, page 230). Brush the inside of the pie shell with beaten egg white to keep it from becoming soggy.

FILLING

1⅓ cups sugar
3 tablespoons cornstarch
2½ cups cranberries
¼ cup water

3 large pears, peeled, cored, and cut into ¼- to ½-inch pieces (about 4 cups diced)
¼ teaspoon ground ginger

Mix the sugar and cornstarch in a 3-quart saucepan. Stir in the cranberries and water. Cook over medium heat, stirring often, until the berries burst and the sauce thickens (4 to 5 minutes). Remove from the heat and stir in the pears and ginger. Pour into the pie shell and top with streusel.

STREUSEL

¾ cup flour
¼ cup butter, softened
½ cup dark brown sugar
2 tablespoons sugar
½ teaspoon cinnamon

Mix the flour, butter, brown sugar, sugar, and cinnamon with your fingers or a fork until crumbly. Sprinkle over the top of the pie.

Bake the pie at 400°F for approximately 45 minutes or until the pears are soft and cranberries cooked. Check after 30 minutes and cover loosely with foil if the streusel gets too brown.

NOTE: I prefer Bosc pears, but any fresh pears work. Ripe Bartlett pears may take a little less time to cook.

❧ Cranberry Cheese Pie

Preheat the oven to 400°F.

CRUST

Prepare a 10-inch graham cracker crust (recipe, page 229). Bake the crust at 400°F for 6 minutes. Remove from the oven and let cool slightly.

FILLING

Turn down the oven to 350°F.

$1\frac{1}{2}$ cups whole
    cranberries
$\frac{3}{4}$ plus $\frac{1}{3}$ cup sugar
$\frac{1}{4}$ cup water
1 pound cream cheese,
    softened

3 eggs
1 teaspoon vanilla
    Whipped cream (optional)

Mix the cranberries, ¾ cup sugar, and water in a 2-quart saucepan. Bring to a boil and cook, stirring, until the cranberries burst and make a thick sauce. Set aside.

Beat the cream cheese until smooth in a large mixing bowl. Beat the eggs, ⅓ cup sugar, and vanilla together in another bowl for 2 minutes. Gradually beat the egg mixture into the cream cheese. When smooth, stir in the cranberry mixture. Pour into the pie shell. Bake at 350°F for 30 to 35 minutes or until set. Decorate with whipped cream piped around the outside edge of the pie. Serve at room temperature or slightly chilled.

❧ Pumpkin or Squash Pie

Pumpkin pie is a favorite at our house. I use sugar pumpkins when they are available, and butternut or blue Hubbard squash when they aren't. I steam the peeled chunks of squash or pumpkin, but boiling or baking is also fine (see cooking methods for pumpkin, page 174). Many people bake unpeeled chunks of pumpkin or squash and then scrape the cooked flesh from the peel, but I prefer to peel it first. It is important to drain the pumpkin or squash thoroughly so the pie won't be wet. If the squash or pumpkin seems overly moist, I press out more liquid while it is still in the colander after draining. Rather than purée the vegetable, I whip it with my electric mixer for a better texture.

Preheat the oven to 425°F.

CRUST

Prepare an unbaked 9-inch pie shell (recipe, page 228). Brush the inside with slightly beaten egg white.

FILLING

2 eggs	¹/₂ teaspoon salt
1 cup milk	1 teaspoon cinnamon
¹/₂ cup light cream	³/₄ teaspoon nutmeg
1¹/₂ cups peeled, cooked, and mashed pumpkin or squash	¹/₂ teaspoon ginger
¹/₃ cup lightly packed dark brown sugar	¹/₄ teaspoon cloves
¹/₄ cup sugar	Whipped cream (optional)

Beat the eggs in a large mixing bowl, then add the remaining ingredients and mix thoroughly. Pour into the pie shell. Bake at 425°F for 20 minutes. Reduce the heat to 350°F and continue to bake for 40 to 45 minutes longer or until the filling has set. Serve at room temperature or chilled, topped with whipped cream.

NOTE: Leftover pie should be refrigerated.

❧ Pumpkin or Squash Custard Pie

Pumpkin pie too spicy for you? Try this milder custard pie for a change. Use either pumpkin or squash.

Preheat the oven to 425°F.

CRUST

Prepare an unbaked 9-inch pie shell (recipe page 228). Brush the inside with slightly beaten egg white.

FILLING

1 cup light cream	1 teaspoon vanilla
1 cup milk	3/4 teaspoon nutmeg
4 eggs	1 cup cooked and puréed, or
1/2 cup sugar	whipped, pumpkin or squash
1/2 teaspoon salt	

Scald the cream and milk together and set aside.

Beat the eggs in a mixing bowl, then stir in the sugar, salt, vanilla, nutmeg, and pumpkin. Stir in the milk and cream, and pour into the pie shell. If desired, sprinkle a little additional ground nutmeg over the top. Bake at 425°F for 15 minutes. Reduce the heat to 350°F and continue to bake for 25 to 30 minutes longer or until the custard tests done with a knife. (When you insert the knife into the custard, it comes out clean.) Serve at room temperature or slightly chilled.

NOTE: Leftover pie should be refrigerated.

✵ Parsnip Pie

I was never a lover of parsnips, but once I started to use them for baking, I found that I enjoy the flavor. Add more spice to the pie if you like, but I feel it detracts from the sweet parsnip taste. When you use spring parsnips, which tend to be sweeter, you may want to cut down some on the sugar.

Preheat the oven to 375°F.

CRUST

Prepare a 9-inch pie shell (recipe, page 228). Bake it at 375°F for 5 minutes or brush the inside with slightly beaten egg white.

Turn up the oven to 400°F.

FILLING

2 eggs	1/3 cup sugar
1 3/4 cups light cream	1/2 teaspoon salt
1 1/2 cups peeled, cooked, and puréed, or whipped parsnips	1 1/4 teaspoons cinnamon
1/3 cup lightly packed dark brown sugar	1/4 teaspoon nutmeg
	1/4 teaspoon ginger
	Whipped cream (optional)

Place all the ingredients in a large mixing bowl and beat together with an eggbeater or on low speed with an electric mixer until well mixed. Pour into the pie shell and bake at 400°F for 50 to 55 minutes or until the center is set. Serve at room temperature or chilled, topped with whipped cream.

NOTE: Leftover pie should be refrigerated.

✵ Strawberry Shortcake

I think the secret to good strawberry shortcake is unchilled strawberries at room temperature. Bake your shortcake at the last minute so it will still be warm, fill it with strawberries, and top it with whipped cream. No one will be able to resist sampling.

Preheat the oven to 450°F. Grease an 8-inch round layer cake pan.

SHORTCAKE

2 cups flour	3 tablespoons solid vegetable
2 tablespoons sugar	shortening
3½ teaspoons baking powder	⅔ cup milk
1 teaspoon salt	1 teaspoon butter, softened
3 tablespoons butter, softened	

Sift the flour, sugar, baking powder, and salt together twice. Cut the 3 tablespoons butter and shortening into the flour mixture with a pastry blender or two knives until it resembles coarse cornmeal. Stir the milk into the flour and shortening mixture with a fork. Turn the dough onto a floured surface and knead it a few times until smooth. Divide the dough in half and pat one half into the greased pan (or roll with a rolling pin to fit the pan). Spread the teaspoon of butter over this layer (so layers will split easily). Pat the second layer over the first (or roll to fit). Bake at 450°F for about 20 minutes or until browned and baked between the layers.

STRAWBERRIES

1 quart strawberries	½ cup sugar (or to taste)

While the shortcake is baking, wash, hull, and mash the strawberries. Stir in the sugar and set aside until ready to serve.

WHIPPED CREAM

½ cup heavy cream	½ teaspoon vanilla
2 teaspoons sugar	

Whip the cream with a whisk or egg beater until it is quite thick. Add the sugar and vanilla and continue beating until the cream reaches the desired stiffness.

Remove the shortcake from the oven and place it on a deep serving platter. Lift off the top layer and set aside. Spoon half the strawberries on the bottom layer. Add the top layer and cover with the remaining berries. Top with whipped cream. Cut into six pie-shaped wedges.

NOTE: The shortcake can also be baked as biscuits for individual servings.

❧ Cranberry-Apple Cake

SERVES 8

I don't know quite what to call this concoction, so cake will have to do. It's not something you'd use as a regular cake (as in birthday), but rather a dessert for the day you have unexpected company or never got around to making dessert. It is best served warm with ice cream — a last-minute dessert.

Preheat the oven to 350°F. Grease and flour an 8-inch-square baking pan.

1 cup coarsely chopped cranberries

3 tablespoons sugar

2 tablespoons butter or margarine, softened

2/3 cup lightly packed dark brown sugar

2 eggs

1 cup flour

2 teaspoons baking powder

1/2 teaspoon salt

1/2 teaspoon cinnamon

1/4 teaspoon nutmeg

2 cups peeled, thinly sliced apples

Mix the cranberries and sugar and set aside. Beat the butter, brown sugar, and eggs together in a large bowl with an electric mixer until smooth. Sift the flour, baking powder, salt, cinnamon, and nutmeg together and beat them into the egg mixture until well blended. Stir the cranberry mixture and apples into the batter until the fruit is coated with the batter, which should be very thick. Spread the batter in the prepared pan. Bake at 350°F for about 35 minutes. Serve warm with ice cream.

✣ Carrot Cake

This old standby is always welcome. I like it with Cream Cheese Frosting (recipe, page 264), but plain vanilla Butter Frosting (recipe, page 263) also goes well.

Preheat the oven to 350°F. Grease and flour an 8-by-11-inch baking pan.

3 eggs	1 teaspoon salt
1 cup sugar	2 teaspoons cinnamon
1 cup oil	1/2 teaspoon nutmeg or mace
1 2/3 cups flour	2 1/2 cups peeled and grated
1 1/2 teaspoons baking soda	carrots
1 1/2 teaspoons baking powder	1/2 cup chopped nuts

Beat the eggs slightly in a large bowl with an electric mixer. Add the sugar and continue to beat until the mixture is thick and light in color (1 to 2 minutes). Gradually beat in the oil. Sift the flour, baking soda, baking powder, salt, cinnamon, and nutmeg together and stir them into the egg mixture. Stir in the carrots and nuts. Pour into the prepared pan and bake at 350°F for 40 to 45 minutes. Cool before frosting.

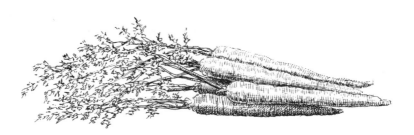

❧ Winter Squash Cake

SERVES 12

I serve this cake at the farm very often and always get raves. One time a little girl about eight years old came back for seconds and then brought her mother over to get the recipe because it was the "best cake" she had ever had. I'm not sure it's the best cake I've ever had, but it certainly is good, and you can make it with any cooked, mashed winter squash or pumpkin.

Preheat the oven to 350°F. Grease a 9-by-13-inch baking pan.

4 eggs	2 teaspoons baking powder
1½ cups sugar	1 teaspoon baking soda
1 cup vegetable oil	1 teaspoon salt
1¾ cups cooked and mashed squash or pumpkin	2 teaspoons cinnamon
2 cups flour	½ teaspoon nutmeg

Beat the eggs well in a large mixing bowl. Add the sugar, oil, and squash and continue to beat until thoroughly mixed. Sift the dry ingredients together and beat them in. Pour the batter into the prepared pan. Bake at 350°F for about 35 minutes. Cool, then cover with Butter Frosting (recipe, page 263).

❧ Zucchini Fudge Cake

SERVES 8 TO 10

Obviously, this cake does not taste like zucchini. But it is deliciously moist and chocolaty, and it's fun to ask people to guess the secret ingredient. I was flattered when Sue Bearce, who works in the fields (picking zucchini, along with many other vegetables), requested it for her birthday.

Preheat the oven to 350°F. Grease a 9-inch-square cake pan.

2/3 cup vegetable oil
1 cup sugar
3 eggs
1 teaspoon vanilla
3 ounces unsweetened
  chocolate, melted and
  slightly cool
1/3 cup milk

1 1/2 cups flour
2 teaspoons baking powder
1 teaspoon baking soda
1/2 teaspoon cinnamon
1 teaspoon salt
2 cups unpeeled, coarsely
  grated zucchini

Beat the oil, sugar, and eggs with an electric mixer until smooth. Add the vanilla, chocolate, and milk and beat until well blended. Sift together the flour, baking powder, baking soda, cinnamon, and salt. Add this to the liquid mixture and beat until smooth. Stir in the grated zucchini and pour into the prepared pan. Bake at 350°F for approximately 45 minutes. Cool, then cover with Butter Frosting (recipe, page 263).

Zucchini Spice Cake

Simple to make, the cake may be served unfrosted in squares, with or without ice cream. It is very spicy and somewhat like gingerbread.

Preheat the oven to 350°F. Grease an 8-inch-square baking pan.

1 cup lightly packed dark
  brown sugar
2 tablespoons sugar
2/3 cup vegetable oil
2 teaspoons vanilla
2 eggs
1 1/2 cups flour
1 teaspoon baking powder

1/2 teaspoon baking soda
3/4 teaspoon salt
1 1/2 teaspoons cinnamon
3/4 teaspoon nutmeg
1/4 teaspoon cloves
1/4 teaspoon ginger
1 1/2 cups coarsely grated
  zucchini (lightly packed)

Beat the brown sugar, sugar, oil, vanilla, and eggs in a large bowl with an electric mixer, until very well blended. Sift together the flour, baking powder, baking soda, salt, cinnamon, nutmeg, cloves, and ginger and beat them into the egg mixture. Stir in the zucchini. Spoon into the prepared pan. The batter should be very thick, but the zucchini provides liquid as it bakes. Bake at 350°F for 40 to 45 minutes. Leave unfrosted or cover with Butter or Cream Cheese Frosting (recipes, pages 263 and 264).

❧ Blueberry and Peach Streusel Squares

MAKES 12 SQUARES

These squares don't turn out picture perfect, but they do taste good. Serve them slightly warm, with ice cream. They're even good cold, but they aren't finger food so plan to serve them with a fork.

Preheat the oven to 350°F. Butter a shallow 8-by-11-inch (2-quart) baking pan.

1 cup lightly packed dark
  brown sugar
½ cup butter or margarine,
  softened
2 cups flour
1 teaspoon baking powder
1 teaspoon cinnamon

½ teaspoon salt
1½ cups blueberries
2½ cups peeled, sliced peaches
⅓ cup sugar
¼ teaspoon nutmeg

Cream the brown sugar and butter together. Sift the flour, baking powder, cinnamon, and salt together and beat them into the sugar and butter mixture with an electric mixer. The result should be crumbly, like streusel. Measure out and set aside 1¼ cups of the streusel mixture. Firmly press the remaining streusel mixture on the bottom of the prepared pan to make a crust.

Mix the blueberries, peaches, sugar, and nutmeg in a large bowl. Add the remaining 1¼ cups of the streusel mixture and stir until the fruit is coated. Spoon it over the crust as evenly as possible. Bake at 350°F for approximately 45 minutes. Cool slightly before cutting into squares.

❧ Carrot-Orange Squares

MAKES 24 TO 32 SQUARES, DEPENDING ON HOW YOU CUT THEM

These moist squares have a brownie-like consistency. Unlike carrot cake, which is made with raw carrots, they are made with cooked carrots. Top with an orange glaze instead of frosting.

Preheat the oven to 350°F. Grease and flour a 9-by-13-inch baking pan.

SQUARES

1/2 cup butter or margarine, softened
3/4 cup sugar
1 cup peeled, cooked, and mashed or puréed carrots (scant pound)
1 egg
2 cups flour
2 teaspoons baking powder
1 teaspoon salt
1/2 teaspoon allspice
1/4 teaspoon cinnamon
1/3 cup orange juice
1 teaspoon grated orange peel
1/2 cup flaked coconut
1/3 cup chopped walnuts

Cream the butter and sugar together. Add the carrots and egg and beat with an electric mixer until very well blended. Sift the flour, baking powder, salt, allspice, and cinnamon together and beat them into the carrot mixture. Beat in the orange juice and peel, and stir in the coconut and walnuts. Spread the batter evenly in the prepared pan. Bake at 350°F for about 35 minutes.

GLAZE

3 tablespoons orange juice
3/4 teaspoon grated orange peel
2 cups confectioners sugar

Mix all the ingredients, and spread on the cake when it is almost cool. Sprinkle the top with grated raw carrot, if desired. Cut into squares when completely cool.

❧ Winter Squash or Pumpkin Cheesecake Squares

MAKES 24 TO 32 SQUARES, DEPENDING ON HOW YOU CUT THEM

Preheat the oven to 350°F.

CRUST

Prepare a graham cracker crust (recipe, page 229), adding ½ teaspoon ground cinnamon to the crumbs. Spread the crust mixture on the bottom of a shallow 9-by-13-inch baking pan. Pack down lightly to make a bottom crust. Bake at 350°F for 10 minutes.

FILLING

  3 eggs
⅔ cup sugar
  1 pound cream cheese,
     softened
1⅓ cups cooked and puréed
     squash or pumpkin

¼ teaspoon cinnamon
⅛ teaspoon nutmeg
⅛ teaspoon cloves
 2 cups sour cream
 2 tablespoons sugar

Beat the eggs in a bowl with an electric mixer for 2 minutes. Gradually beat in the ⅔ cup sugar. Beat the cream cheese and squash together in another bowl. Gradually beat the egg mixture into the cream cheese and squash mixture. Add the cinnamon, nutmeg, and cloves and beat until well blended. Pour the filling over the crust. Bake at 350°F for 30 to 35 minutes. Let cool for 5 minutes.

Mix the sour cream and 2 tablespoons sugar. After 5 minutes spread the mixture on the squares, sprinkle with ground cinnamon, and return to the oven. Bake for 8 minutes longer. Cool completely before cutting into squares.

NOTE: Leftovers should be refrigerated.

❧ Rhubarb Crisp

Rhubarb Crisp, simple and quick to make, is a perfect last-minute dessert, as it's best served warm.

Preheat the oven to 350°F. Butter an 8- or 9-inch-square baking pan.

FILLING

7 cups ½-inch slices rhubarb	3 tablespoons flour
1¼ cups sugar	½ teaspoon cinnamon

Mix the rhubarb, sugar, flour, and cinnamon and spread in the prepared pan.

STREUSEL

½ cup flour	2 tablespoons sugar
1 cup quick-cooking oatmeal	½ teaspoon cinnamon
½ cup lightly packed light or dark brown sugar	⅓ cup butter or margarine, softened

Mix the flour, oatmeal, sugars, cinnamon, and butter with a fork or your fingers until crumbly. Sprinkle over the rhubarb.

Bake at 350°F for 45 to 50 minutes or until the rhubarb is soft and the streusel topping brown. Serve warm with ice cream or light cream.

ℒ Indian Pudding with Apples

SERVES 6 TO 8

Nothing is more typically New England than Indian Pudding. I add apples for a perfect autumn dessert.

Preheat the oven to 300°F. Butter a deep 2-quart casserole.

4 cups milk
⅓ cup yellow cornmeal
½ cup molasses
⅓ cup sugar
1 egg, slightly beaten
1 tablespoon butter

¼ teaspoon cinnamon
¼ teaspoon salt
½ teaspoon ginger
2 cups sliced apples
 (2 medium, sliced)

Scald 3 cups of the milk in a 2-quart saucepan. Remove from the heat and stir in the cornmeal and molasses. Return the pan to the heat and cook, stirring, for 2 to 3 minutes over medium, until slightly thick. Remove the pan from the heat and stir in the sugar, beaten egg, butter, cinnamon, salt, ginger, and apples. When well mixed, pour into the prepared casserole. Bake, uncovered, at 300°F for 30 minutes. Pour the remaining 1 cup of cold milk over the pudding. Do not stir. Continue to bake for 1½ hours longer.

Serve warm with ice cream (coffee ice cream is especially good on Indian Pudding), whipped cream, or my favorite, plain light cream.

❦ Apple Bread Pudding

SERVES ABOUT 6

A treat served with ice cream or plain cream while still warm, this pudding is custardy, and even people who hate bread pudding gobble it up.

Preheat the oven to 350°F. Butter a deep 1½-quart casserole lightly.

2 cups milk
⅓ cup sugar
¼ cup butter or margarine
2 cups lightly packed ½-inch-cubes stale white bread (about 3 slices)
3 eggs, slightly beaten

2 cups apples in ½-inch cubes
½ cup seedless raisins
¼ teaspoon salt
1 teaspoon cinnamon
½ teaspoon nutmeg
½ teaspoon vanilla

Scald the milk. Remove from the heat and add the sugar and butter, stirring until the butter melts and the sugar dissolves.

Place the bread cubes in a mixing bowl. Pour the milk mixture over the bread and let stand for 5 minutes. Stir in the eggs, apple, raisins (saving a few), salt, cinnamon, nutmeg, and vanilla. Pour into the prepared casserole and sprinkle the reserved raisins over the top. Place the casserole in a shallow pan filled with hot water to a depth of ½ inch. Bake at 350°F for approximately 1 hour or until the center is set. Insert a knife into the pudding as you would test a custard. When the knife comes out clean, the pudding is done.

Serve either warm or cold with whipped cream, ice cream, or plain light cream.

❧ Baked Apples

Baked apples may be an old-fashioned dessert, but they are still very much in favor. Here are three recipes: the first, Simple Baked Apples, the second, Baked Apples Stuffed with Raisins and Nuts, and the last, for adults, Baked Apples with Rum.

Each recipe is for 5 or 6 medium apples peeled one-third to halfway down from the stem end and cored. Cortlands hold their shape best, but other varieties, with the exception of tart green ones, are good.

Simple Baked Apples

Preheat the oven to 350°F.

⅓ to ½ cup sugar (depending on variety of apple)
1 cup water
¼ teaspoon ground cinnamon

Few drops red food coloring (for pink apples — optional)

Peel and core the apples. Place them in a shallow baking dish. Mix all the ingredients in a small saucepan. Bring to a boil over high heat and boil for 1 minute. Pour the hot syrup over the apples. Bake, uncovered, at 350°F, basting often, for about 45 minutes or until the apples are fork-tender.

Serve warm or cold, placing each apple and some of the remaining syrup in individual serving dishes and topping with ice cream, whipped cream, or light cream.

Baked Apples Stuffed with Raisins and Walnuts

Preheat the oven to 350°F.

½ cup chopped walnuts
½ cup seedless raisins
⅓ to ½ cup light brown sugar (depending on tartness of apples)

1 cup water
¼ teaspoon cinnamon
Dash nutmeg

Peel and core the apples. Place them in a shallow baking dish. Pack the cavities of the apples with a mixture of walnuts and raisins. Mix the sugar, water, cinnamon, and nutmeg in a small saucepan. Bring to a boil over high heat and boil for 1 minute. Pour the hot syrup over the apples. Cover them loosely with foil. Bake at 350°F for 15 minutes. Uncover and continue to bake for 30 to 40 minutes longer, basting often, until the apples are fork-tender. Serve warm or cold, as with Simple Baked Apples.

Baked Apples with Rum

Preheat the oven to 350°F.

⅓ cup chopped nuts
⅓ cup seedless raisins
⅓ cup flaked coconut
½ cup lightly packed dark
  brown sugar
1 cup water

¼ teaspoon vanilla
¼ teaspoon cinnamon
1 teaspoon butter
2 tablespoons rum (preferably dark)

Peel and core the apples. Place them in a shallow baking dish. Mix the nuts, raisins, and coconut and pack the cavities of the apples with the mixture. Mix the remaining ingredients in a small saucepan. Bring to a boil over high heat and boil for 1 minute. Pour the hot syrup over the apples. Cover them loosely with foil and bake at 350°F for 15 minutes. Uncover and continue to bake for 30 to 40 minutes longer, basting often, until the apples are fork-tender. Serve warm or cold, as with Simple Baked Apples.

✣ Pears Poached with Cranberries

SERVES 6

By choice, Don Wilson did most of the testing and sampling of this dessert. Despite his sweet tooth (and the natural tartness of cranberries), he claimed that he would much rather have these pears than pie or cake after a meal.

1½ *cups whole cranberries*
¾ *cup water*
⅔ *to 1 cup sugar (or to taste)*
1 *teaspoon vanilla*

3 *medium pears (about 1½ pounds, halved, peeled, and cored)*

Cook the cranberries, water, sugar, and vanilla in a 3-quart saucepan, uncovered, over medium heat until the sugar dissolves and the cranberries burst. Add the pear halves and simmer, covered, for 20 minutes or until the pears are fairly tender. Uncover and simmer for 15 to 20 minutes longer, basting occasionally, until the pears are very soft but still in one piece and the sauce has thickened. Remove from the heat and let the pears cool in the syrup. Serve the pear halves at room temperature or slightly chilled, surrounded with sauce and topped with ice cream or whipped cream.

NOTE: Any pears will work as long as they are not too ripe. Anjou and Bartlett take less time to cook than Bosc, which give excellent flavor, so adjust the cooking time accordingly.

❧ Cranberry Sundae Sauce

I had a hard time trying to decide what to call this very strange sauce. Served warm over vanilla ice cream, it makes a quick, easy, and elegant dessert. And served chilled, it makes an interesting complement to poultry.

1 cup sugar
1½ tablespoons cornstarch
1 cup water
2 cups whole cranberries
¾ cup seedless raisins

1 tablespoon butter
1 teaspoon vanilla
½ cup chopped walnuts or pecans

Stir the sugar and cornstarch together in a 2-quart saucepan. Add the water, cranberries, and raisins. Cover and bring to a boil over medium-high heat. Lower the heat and simmer, stirring often, until the cranberries are cooked and the sauce has thickened (about 5 to 7 minutes). Mash cranberries that remain whole. Remove from the heat and stir in the butter, vanilla, and chopped nuts.

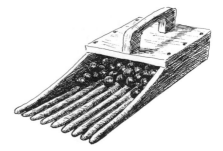

❧ Dessert in a Pumpkin Shell

SERVES 6 TO 8

Impress your guests or family with dessert baked in a pumpkin shell. Bring it to the table filled with gingerbread, spice cake (mixes are fine), or firm bread pudding. Bring it to the table whole, cut it into wedges, and serve, pumpkin and all. The cooked pumpkin, except for the skin, may be eaten along with the filling.

Preheat the oven to 350°F.

1 sugar pumpkin (3 to 5 pounds) or 2 smaller ones
1 tablespoon butter
1 tablespoon brown sugar

¼ teaspoon cinnamon
Gingerbread or spice cake batter, or bread pudding mixture

Cut off the pumpkin top straight across and clean out the pumpkin thoroughly. Put the butter, brown sugar, and cinnamon in the pumpkin shell. Place the shell in the oven and heat for 20 to 30 minutes. Brush the butter and sugar around the inside of the shell several times while it heats.

When the pumpkin shell is hot, brush the butter and sugar around the inside once more and pour out the remaining syrup and accumulated juices. Add the batter, filling the pumpkin two-thirds full to allow room for expansion. Better to cook two small pumpkins than to have the batter spill out over your oven. (I speak from experience!)

Bake at 350°F until done. Allow more time than the filling recipe usually takes. For instance, a gingerbread mix that calls for 30 minutes baking time takes 45 minutes to 1 hour. The pumpkin will be soft and ready to eat when the filling is baked. Cool slightly. Decorate the top with whipped cream or cut the pumpkin into wedges and serve ice cream beside each wedge.

NOTE: Use a short, fat (squatty) pumpkin so there is a wide opening and more batter is exposed to the oven heat.

🍰 Butter Frosting

MAKES ENOUGH TO FROST THE TOP AND SIDES OF A 9-BY-13-INCH CAKE

1 pound confectioners sugar
5 tablespoons butter or
  margarine, softened
¼ cup (or less) hot milk

¾ teaspoon vanilla
Food coloring (optional)
Chopped nuts (optional)

Place the sugar and butter in a mixing bowl and beat them together with an electric mixer on low speed. Gradually beat in the hot milk, a little at a time, until the frosting is of spreading consistency. Stir in the vanilla and food coloring. Top the frosting with chopped nuts.

NOTE: For a change, substitute ¼ teaspoon peppermint flavoring for the vanilla when frosting a chocolate cake.

❧ Cream Cheese Frosting

MAKES ENOUGH TO FROST A 9-INCH-SQUARE OR 8-BY-11-INCH CAKE

3 ounces cream cheese, softened
1 tablespoon butter, softened
2 cups confectioners sugar
  Dash salt

1 to 2 tablespoons hot milk
½ teaspoon vanilla
  Chopped nuts or finely
  grated raw carrot
  (optional)

Beat the cream cheese, butter, sugar, and salt together with an electric mixer or spoon until well blended. Beat in the hot milk, 1 tablespoon at a time, and vanilla until the frosting is of spreading consistency. Top the frosting with chopped nuts or carrot (for Carrot Cake — recipe, page 249).

❧ Whipped Cream

This recipe makes enough sweet whipped cream to pipe around the edge of a pie or to put a spoonful on each slice.

½ cup heavy cream
 2 teaspoons sugar

½ teaspoon vanilla

Using an electric mixer, whisk, or eggbeater, whip the cream until quite thick. Add the sugar and vanilla and continue to beat until the cream reaches desired stiffness. Refrigerate if you aren't going to use it immediately.

Index